Preface

The Army is attempting to transform itself from a force designed primarily to fight large and protracted wars in a limited number of locations to one capable of reacting rapidly to crises anywhere in the world. In its endeavor to make its combat units more versatile and agile, the Army is planning to replace its heavy, aging armored combat vehicles with newer, lighter systems that it expects will be as lethal and survivable as the vehicles they are replacing. Several types of manned vehicles as well as unmanned aerial and ground vehicles, missile launchers, and communications links would be developed and procured within a single program known as the Future Combat Systems (FCS) program.

This study by the Congressional Budget Office (CBO), which was prepared at the request of the Ranking Member of the Tactical Air and Land Forces Subcommittee of the House Committee on Armed Services, considers the near- and long-term implications of the FCS program. It also examines several alternatives for modernizing the Army's armored forces and estimates the costs and savings associated with those options as well as their effects on the Army's fleet of armored vehicles and the ability of its armored units to deploy overseas. In keeping with CBO's mandate to provide objective, impartial analysis, the report makes no recommendations.

Frances M. Lussier of CBO's National Security Division prepared the study under the general supervision of J. Michael Gilmore. The author would like to thank Michael J. Bennett of CBO for his assistance in fact-checking the document as well as former Department of Defense official Thomas P. Christie for his comments and Army personnel for their help. (The assistance of external participants implies no responsibility for the final product, which rests solely with the author and CBO.) Victoria Liu, also of CBO, reviewed the manuscript, and Arlene Holen, Sarah Jennings, Jo Ann Vines, Jason Wheelock, and Christopher Williams provided comments on earlier drafts of the study.

Leah Mazade edited the report, and Christine Bogusz proofread it. Cindy Cleveland produced drafts of the text and tables, and Maureen Costantino designed the cover and prepared the study for publication. Lenny Skutnik produced the initial printed copies. This publication and others may be found at www.cbo.gov.

Donald B. Marron
Acting Director

August 2006

Contents

Summary   *xi*

1

The Army's Heavy Forces and Armored Vehicles   *1*

Overview of the Army's Armored Vehicle Fleet at the End of 2003   *2*

Issues Regarding Today's Armored Forces and Vehicles   *5*

2

Description of the Army's Modularity Initiative and Future Combat Systems Program   *17*

The Modularity Initiative   *17*

The Future Combat Systems Program   *21*

3

Potential Effects of and Concerns About the Army's Modernization Plans   *29*

How Modernization Plans Would Affect the Army's Budget   *29*

How Modernization Plans Would Affect the Army's Ability to Deploy Units Quickly   *31*

How the Administration's Plan Would Affect the Army's Armored Combat Vehicle Fleet   *32*

Concerns Regarding the Army's FCS Program   *34*

4

Alternative Approaches to Modernizing the Army's Heavy Forces   *47*

Alternative 1. Develop and Procure FCS Components That Will Collect and Disseminate Information   *47*

Alternative 2. Develop and Procure FCS Components That Will Enhance the Army's Long-Range Strike Capability   *54*

Alternative 3. Emphasize Investment in New Manned Combat Vehicles   *57*

Alternative 4. Develop a Scaled-Down FCS Network and Integrate It with Existing Systems   *60*

iii

A Description and History of the Army's Current Armored Vehicles *63*

CBO's Methods for Estimating Airlift Requirements *71*

Definitions of Technology Readiness Levels and Assessments of Critical Technologies for the Army's Future Combat Systems Program *73*

Methods Used to Estimate Costs *81*

Tables

S-1. FCS Components and Current Counterparts in Combat Brigades — *xiii*

S-2. Comparing the Army's Modular Heavy Combat Brigades and Brigades Equipped with Future Combat Systems — *xviii*

S-3. Time Needed to Deploy Equipment of Combat Units to East Africa — *xix*

S-4. Emphasis of and FCS Components Included in Alternatives — *xxi*

S-5. Total Acquisition Costs from 2007 to 2025 for the Administration's Plan and Alternatives — *xxii*

1-1. Characteristics of Models of the M1 Abrams Tank in 2003 — *3*

1-2. Characteristics of Models of the M2/M3 Bradley Fighting Vehicle in 2003 — *6*

1-3. Characteristics of Models of M113-Based Vehicles in 2003 — *7*

1-4. Characteristics of Models of the M109 Self-Propelled Howitzer in 2003 — *9*

1-5. Army Units Equipped with Armored Vehicles in 2003 — *10*

1-6. Armored Vehicles Needed to Equip and Support the Army's Heavy Units in 2003 — *12*

1-7. Comparing the Army's Light Infantry, Airborne, and Armored Units in 2003 — *13*

2-1. Comparing the Army's Premodular and Modular Combat Force Structures — *18*

2-2. Comparing the Army's Premodular Heavy Brigade Combat Teams and Modular Heavy Combat Brigades — *19*

2-3. Armored Combat Vehicles Needed to Equip and Support the Army's Modular Heavy Combat Brigades in 2011 — *20*

2-4. FCS Replacements for Armored Vehicles in the Army's Modular Heavy Combat Brigades — *23*

3-1. Planned New Components for an FCS-Equipped Brigade — *30*

3-2. Total Costs for the Army's Modularity Initiative — *32*

3-3. Selected Items That the Army Plans to Buy to Implement Its Modularity Initiative — *33*

3-4. Upgrades Included in the Administration's Plan for 2007 to 2016 — *34*

3-5. Comparing the Army's Premodular Heavy Brigade Combat Teams, Modular Heavy Combat Brigades, and Brigades Equipped with Future Combat Systems — *35*

3-6. Time Needed to Deploy Equipment of Combat Units to East Africa — *36*

4-1. Alternatives to the Administration's Current Plan for the FCS Program — *48*

Tables (Continued)

4-2.   Procurement of FCS Components Under the Administration's Plan and Under Alternative 1   *49*

4-3.   Total Acquisition Costs from 2007 to 2025 for the Administration's Plan and Alternatives   *51*

4-4.   Time Needed to Deploy Equipment of Combat Units to East Africa   *53*

4-5.   Procurement of FCS Components Under the Administration's Plan and Under Alternative 2   *55*

4-6.   Procurement of FCS Components Under the Administration's Plan and Under Alternative 3   *58*

A-1.   Characteristics of Models of the Abrams (M1) Tank   *67*

A-2.   Characteristics of Models of the Bradley Infantry (M2) and Cavalry (M3) Fighting Vehicles   *68*

A-3.   Characteristics of Models of the M113-Based Family of Vehicles   *69*

A-4.   Characteristics of Models of the M109 Self-Propelled Howitzer   *70*

B-1.   CBO's Estimates of Maximum Airfield Capacity   *72*

C-1.   Definitions and Descriptions of Technology Readiness Levels   *74*

C-2.   Technology Readiness Levels of Critical Technologies for the FCS Program in May 2003   *77*

C-3.   Status of Critical Technologies for the FCS Program As Assessed After May 2003   *78*

D-1.   Rates of Historical Cost Growth for Military Systems   *83*

Figures

S-1.   Annual Costs of the Administration's Plan for the Future Combat Systems Program and Alternatives   *xiv*

S-2.   Effect of the Administration's Plan for the FCS Program and Alternatives on the Average Age of the Army's Active Armored Combat Vehicle Fleet   *xvii*

1-1.   The Army's Armored Combat Vehicle Fleet, 1980 to 2003   *2*

1-2.   Abrams Tank   *4*

1-3.   Bradley Fighting Vehicle   *5*

1-4.   M113 Armored Personnel Carrier   *5*

1-5.   M109 Self-Propelled Howitzer   *8*

Figures (Continued)

1-6.   Average Age of the Army's Armored Combat Vehicles, 1990 to 2003   *10*

1-7.   Time Needed to Deploy Equipment of Combat Units from the Continental United States to East Africa   *14*

1-8.   Requirements and Inventories for the Army's Armored Combat Vehicles in 2003   *15*

2-1.   Manned FCS Vehicles   *22*

2-2.   Unmanned FCS Aerial Vehicles   *24*

2-3.   Unmanned FCS Ground Vehicles   *25*

2-4.   Other Unmanned FCS Systems   *26*

2-5.   Disposition of the Army's Heavy Brigades Under the Administration's Plan   *27*

3-1.   Projected Total Annual Investment in the Future Combat Systems Program   *31*

3-2.   Average Age and Composition of the Active Armored Combat Vehicle Fleet   *37*

3-3.   Average Age and Composition of the Armored Combat Vehicle Fleet Under the Administration's Plan   *38*

3-4.   Average Age and Composition of the Active Armored Combat Vehicle Fleet Under the Administration's Plan   *38*

3-5.   Status of Critical Technologies for FCS Components at the End of 2005   *39*

3-6.   The Army's Major Procurement Programs and Budget Through 2025   *40*

3-7.   Estimated Total Annual Costs for the Future Combat Systems Program Including Potential Cost Growth   *43*

3-8.   Average Age of the Active Armored Combat Vehicle Fleet Under the Administration's Plan with Additional Upgrades   *44*

3-9.   Average Age and Composition of the Active Armored Combat Vehicle Fleet with Limited Purchases of FCS Components   *45*

4-1.   Annual Costs of the Administration's Plan for the Future Combat Systems Program and Alternatives   *52*

4-2.   Average Age and Composition of the Active Armored Combat Vehicle Fleet Under All Alternatives   *54*

A-1.   Average Age and Composition of the Army's A1 Abrams Tank Fleet   *63*

A-2.   Average Age and Composition of the Army's M2/M3 Bradley Fighting Vehicle Fleet   *64*

Figures (Continued)

A-3.   Average Age and Composition of the Army's M113-Based Vehicle Fleet   *65*

A-4.   Average Age and Composition of the Army's Fleet of M109 Self-Propelled
        Howitzers   *66*

Summary

Roughly half of the Army's combat forces at the end of 2005 were so-called heavy units—forces that are equipped with armored vehicles and that provide significant firepower. To support those units, the Army maintains a fleet of approximately 28,000 armored vehicles. Now that the Cold War is over, some defense experts have questioned the relevance of such vehicles to the current national security strategy and their continued usefulness (notwithstanding their contributions to recent operations, such as Desert Storm and Iraqi Freedom). The average age of the armored combat vehicle fleet at the end of 2005 was relatively high, and the fleet comprises vehicles designed several decades ago. Moreover, units equipped with the vehicles in the current fleet are too large and too heavy to be moved overseas easily and quickly by the Air Force's C-17s, the most numerous of its long-range transport planes. For all practical purposes, heavy units must be transported overseas by ship—a process that takes weeks.

In today's environment of rapidly evolving conflicts, the Army's goal is to have units that have the combat power of heavy units but that can be transported anywhere in the world in a matter of days. To address concerns about the armored vehicle fleet's aging and the difficulties involved in transporting it—as well as to equip the Army more suitably to conduct operations overseas on short notice using forces based in the United States—the service created the Future Combat Systems (FCS) program in 2000. A major modernization effort, the program is designed in part to develop and purchase vehicles to replace those now in the heavy forces; the new vehicles would be much lighter, thereby easing the deployment of units equipped with them. But the FCS program, poised to develop a total of 18 new systems (including eight manned vehicles to replace those in the Army's current armored fleet) and a network to connect them all will not field any new vehicles until December 2014 at the earliest. Furthermore, because those new vehicles will be expensive, the Army plans to buy relatively small quantities of them each year. As a result, the armored vehicles now in the Army's combat units will not all be replaced by FCS components until after 2035, a prospect that has evoked concerns about the costs of maintaining those older vehicles and upgrading them to prevent their becoming obsolete.

In addition, questions have been raised about the FCS program's technical feasibility and affordability. Some experts doubt that the Army can develop and test the necessary technologies in time to start producing lightweight manned vehicles by 2012—a requisite for meeting the deadline to field them according to the Army's current schedule. Another concern is funding for the quantities of FCS equipment that the Army is now planning to buy. Any reduction in the FCS procurement rate would force the Army to retain its already aging armored vehicles even longer and to invest more funds in their maintenance.

In the analysis presented in this report, the Congressional Budget Office (CBO) examined the current status of the Army's fleet of armored vehicles and assessed the speed of deployment of the service's heavy forces. It also evaluated the FCS program, considering the program's costs as well as its advantages and disadvantages and comparing it with several alternative plans for modernizing the Army's heavy forces.[1] CBO's analysis supports the following observations:

- The FCS program must surmount substantial technical and funding challenges if it is to develop and initially field all of the individual FCS components as currently scheduled—that is, by December 2014.

---

1. A fuller discussion of the four alternatives that CBO evaluated, each of which emphasized different aspects of the FCS program—information collection and sharing (Alternative 1); long-range strike missions (Alternative 2); new vehicular technology (Alternative 3); and integrating the FCS network into existing systems (Alternative 4)—can be found later in this summary.

■ According to the Army's estimates, total annual costs to purchase the various FCS components could approach $10 billion. However, if such costs grew as those of similar programs have in the past, annual costs could reach $16 billion.

■ Moreover, if the Army fielded FCS vehicles according to its current schedule, $1 billion or more of additional funding might be needed annually from 2010 through 2016—and smaller amounts thereafter—to maintain and upgrade the Army's inventory of aging ground combat vehicles.

■ Although one of the main purposes of the FCS program is to speed the movement of Army combat units overseas, replacing the current fleet of armored vehicles with FCS components will not significantly reduce deployment times.

■ Alternatives to the currently planned FCS program that would eliminate all or part of the program's ground vehicles while retaining its communications equipment and, in some cases, its sensors would reduce the program's average annual costs to about $5 billion to $7 billion. Under such alternatives, the Army would incorporate some FCS technologies into its current fleet of armored combat vehicles and upgrade those vehicles at the same time, thereby increasing their capabilities and extending their useful lives. However, if it did so, the Army would forgo potential benefits of the capabilities it now seeks in the FCS program.

Description of the Army's Future Combat Systems Program

The FCS program was first conceived by then Army Chief of Staff General Eric Shinseki to enable the Army to react to overseas crises more quickly and with overwhelming combat power. The service initiated the program to develop a new generation of combat vehicles that would be as lethal and survivable as the heavy weapons it now fields but that would weigh much less, be more easily transported, and require far less logistical support.

According to the Army, the FCS program would greatly enhance the capabilities and agility of its heavy units by developing new systems to replace most of the combat vehicles that currently equip the service's heavy units and by developing and buying several types of unmanned aerial

and ground vehicles to provide remote—and sometimes autonomous—surveillance and protection. Specifically, the Army would develop eight new types of armored vehicles, four classes of unmanned aerial vehicles (UAVs), three types of unmanned ground vehicles, unattended ground sensors, a missile launcher, and intelligent munitions, all of which would be linked by an advanced communications network into an integrated combat system.

Manned FCS Vehicles

The eight new manned vehicles that would be developed through the FCS program are intended to replace the armored vehicles currently assigned to the Army's heavy combat units (see Summary Table 1). The eight variants would share a common chassis and engine as well as other components, which would reduce the logistics burden associated with maintaining them. The vehicles would have new weapons, sensors, and types of protection, making them, according to the Army, more capable than current systems. The FCS vehicles are also being developed to be more fuel efficient; some armored vehicles in the Army's current fleet—notably the Abrams tanks and Bradley fighting vehicles—go less than two miles on a gallon of fuel.

Initially, the Army aimed to develop FCS vehicles that weighed less than 20 tons and that could be transported by the Air Force's C-130 aircraft. However, the weight limit for the initial design of the manned FCS ground vehicles has been relaxed and is now set at 24 tons—which would nevertheless be about one-third of the weight of the latest model of the Abrams tank and roughly three-quarters that of the Bradley fighting vehicle.

Unmanned Aerial and Ground Vehicles

Four classes of unmanned aerial vehicles and three types of unmanned ground vehicles would be developed under the FCS program to provide, along with the manned systems, surveillance, protection, and cargo-carrying capacity. The aerial vehicles would have varying capabilities: for example, the smallest, Class I, UAV would weigh less than 15 pounds, have a range of eight kilometers (km), and be able to stay aloft for about one hour, whereas the largest, Class IV, UAV could weigh more than 3,000 pounds, have a range of 75 km, and be able to stay aloft for up to 24 hours. The three types of unmanned FCS ground vehicles, or robots, are intended in general to lighten the load of individual soldiers by providing continuous surveillance, carrying supplies, or investigating

Summary Table 1.

FCS Components and Current Counterparts in Combat Brigades

Component	Mission	Existing System Being Replaced
Manned Vehicles		
Mounted Combat	Destroy the enemy	Abrams tank
Infantry Carrier	Transport and protect soldiers	Bradley infantry fighting vehicle and M113 armored personnel carrier
Reconnaissance and Surveillance	Scout	Bradley cavalry fighting vehicle
Non-Line-of-Sight Cannon	Provide fire support	M109 howitzer
Recovery and Maintenance	Recover stranded vehicles	M88 recovery vehicle
Command and Control	Transport and protect commanders	M113-based vehicle
Non-Line-of-Sight Mortar	Provide fire support	M113-based vehicle
Medical	Treat and evacuate the wounded	None
Unmanned Ground Vehicles		
Armed Robotic	Perform sentry duty; provide cover	None
Multifunction Utility, Logistics, and Equipment	Carry cargo; detect and counter mines	None
Small Unmanned Ground	Investigate small, confined spaces	None
Unmanned Aerial Vehicles		
Class I	Provide surveillance up to a distance of 8 km	Raven
Class II	Provide surveillance up to a distance of 16 km	None
Class III	Provide surveillance and communications relay up to a distance of 40 km	Shadow
Class IV	Provide surveillance and communications relay up to a distance of 75 km	None
Other		
Non-Line-of-Sight Launch System	Carry out precision attacks up to a distance of 70 km	None
Unattended Ground Sensors	Detect and identify intruders	REMBASS
Intelligent Munitions System	Channel enemy movement	"Smart" land mines

Source: Congressional Budget Office based on data from the Department of the Army; Army Project Manager, Unit of Action, "Future Combat Systems (FCS); 18+1+1 Systems Overview" (September 2005); and Army Training and Doctrine Command (Tradoc), Unit of Action Maneuver Battle Lab and Tradoc System Manager FCS, "Family of Systems Battle Book" (January 31, 2005).

Note: FCS = Future Combat Systems; UAV = unmanned aerial vehicle; km = kilometer; REMBASS = remotely monitored battlefield sensor system.

high-risk areas or locations (for example, tunnels or caves).

Unattended Sensors, Intelligent Munitions, Launchers, and the Network

The remaining hardware systems to be developed under the FCS program include ground sensors, a missile launcher, an intelligent munitions system, and equipment associated with the communications and data-sharing network. The unattended ground sensors are small modules equipped with several different types of sensors that are intended to act as remote sentries and provide early warning of an attack. The intelligent munitions system is based on sophisticated land mines that can self-destruct on command or at a specific time. The ground sensors and the munitions system are designed to be relatively inexpensive and to detect and destroy intruders over a wide area. The non-line-of-sight launch system—a box-shaped launcher equipped with 15 advanced missiles—may be operated remotely or set to operate autonomously; it is intended to carry out rapid-fire attacks on targets at a distance of as much as 70 km.

Summary Figure 1.

Annual Costs of the Administration's Plan for the Future Combat Systems Program and Alternatives

(Billions of 2006 dollars)

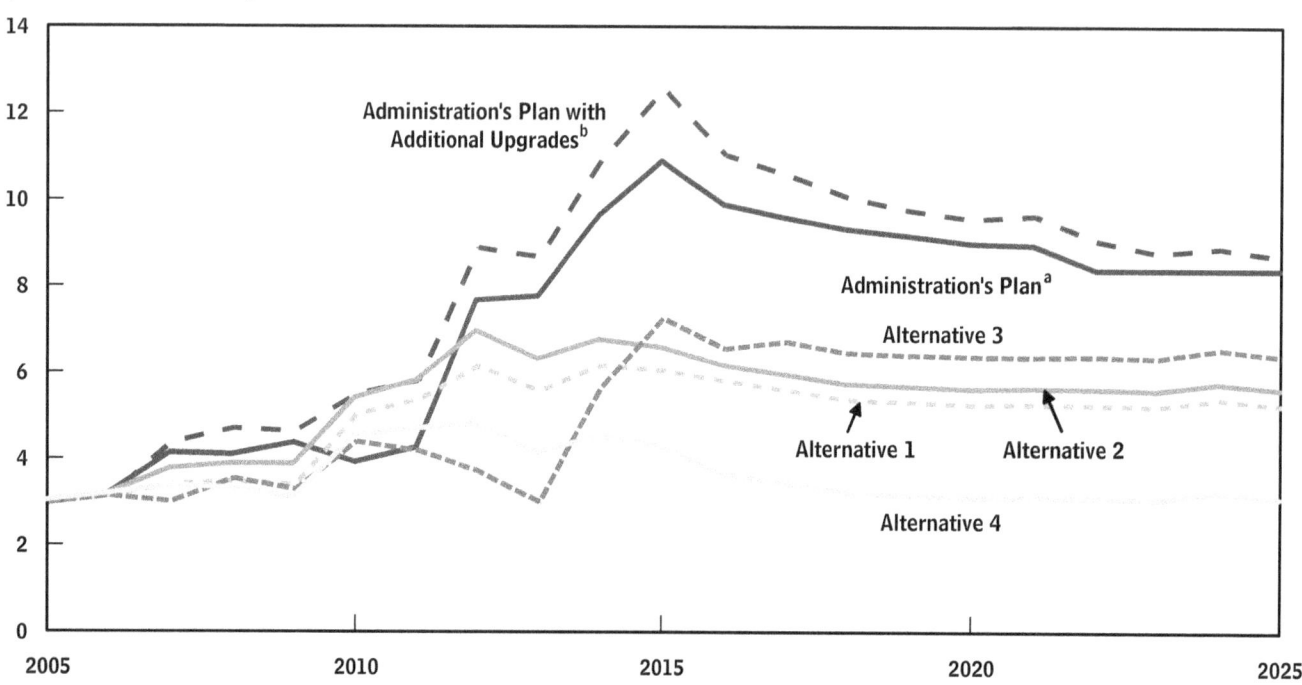

Source: Congressional Budget Office.

Note: See Summary Table 4 for details of the alternatives.

a.   Based on documents submitted with the President's 2007 budget, which includes $6 billion for upgrades to existing systems.

b.   Includes upgrades to Abrams tanks, Bradley fighting vehicles, M113-based vehicles, and M109 howitzers to maintain a relatively constant average age for each fleet of vehicles after 2011.

The final component of the FCS program is the network, which comprises the common operating software that would allow all of the FCS elements to communicate with one another and with other Army systems and to share data. The network also includes the communications and computer systems that are planned to provide secure, reliable access to information collected by the many surveillance sensors in the future FCS-equipped brigade.

Schedule for Fielding FCS Components

Despite the complexity and diversity that the 18 individual FCS components represent, the Army plans to field them all on a very tight schedule. Components would be introduced in stages (which the Army refers to as spinouts, or spirals); fielding would begin in 2010 with the unattended ground sensors, the non-line-of-sight launch

system, and the intelligent munitions system. However, the Army does not expect to field the first combat brigade to be equipped with all 18 systems until December 2014. After that, the service plans to equip its combat brigades with FCS components at a maximum rate of 1.5 brigades per year, purchasing 15 brigades' worth of equipment as part of the first installment—or "increment"—of procurement for the program.[2] Under the current schedule, equipment for the 15th brigade would be purchased in 2023, allowing fielding of those systems in 2026.

---

2.   Procurement of FCS components is often discussed in terms of a brigade's worth of equipment, which includes more than 300 manned vehicles, approximately 230 unmanned ground vehicles, more than 200 UAVs, and numerous additional unattended ground sensors, launch systems, and associated munitions.

Costs of the Army's FCS Program

The FCS program represents by far the biggest single investment that the Army is planning to make during the next 20 years. The research and development (R&D) portion of the program is scheduled to extend through 2016 and cost a total of $21 billion from 2007 to 2016. The Army estimates that total procurement costs for the first 15 brigades' worth of systems will be about $100 billion, or an average unit procurement cost per brigade of $6.7 billion.[3] The Army plans to start its annual purchases of 1.5 brigades' worth of equipment in 2015; as long as the program continues purchases at that rate, from that year on it will require annual funding of $8 billion to $10 billion (see Summary Figure 1).

Concerns About the FCS Program

The Government Accountability Office (GAO) and other defense experts have expressed a number of reservations about the Army's ability to implement the FCS program in its current form. Among their concerns are the technological challenges facing developers of the various systems; the costs of the program, in light of the Army's other funding needs; the condition of the service's current fleet of armored vehicles, which will be retained for several decades until they can be replaced by FCS vehicles; the limited improvement in the speed of Army units' deployment that the fielding of FCS components is likely to bring; and the survivability of FCS vehicles in hostile environments.

Technological Readiness of FCS Components

Defense analysts have questioned whether the planned FCS components will be ready to go into production in 2012. GAO, for example, has criticized the Army's proposed schedule for developing and fielding the 18 systems, given that, according to GAO, it would require developing multiple systems and a network in the same amount of time that the Department of Defense (DoD) typically takes to develop a single advanced system.[4] Also

according to GAO, none of the numerous technologies that are critical to developing the various FCS components—technologies that should have been "mature" before the program entered the system development and demonstration (SDD) phase in 2003—were judged to be so in an independent assessment dated April 2005.[5] Using GAO's criteria, those technologies may not be mature until 2012, when the first FCS component is slated to go into production.

Another technological hurdle is development of the software that will allow all of the new systems to communicate and share data with one another and with the Army's existing systems. At least 34 million lines of software code must be generated—about twice the amount needed for the Joint Strike Fighter, DoD's largest software development effort to date.

The severity of the technological challenges associated with developing all 18 FCS components and the network to link them has already led to increases in the time and funds allotted to FCS development. As the program was first described by General Shinseki in October 1999 and as the schedule stood in November 2002, FCS development would have included a relatively short (three-year) SDD phase starting in the spring of 2003, with all 18 systems slated to enter production by 2006 and to start initial fielding in 2008. Since then, the schedule has been extended by more than six years, and the first unit to be equipped with all 18 systems will not be fielded until December 2014 (fiscal year 2015) at the earliest.

Growth of the FCS Program's Costs

As noted earlier, the Army estimates that the FCS program will require $8 billion to $10 billion annually starting in 2015, when it plans to begin buying 1.5 brigades' worth of equipment per year. During the preceding five years, the program will have consumed increasingly larger shares of the Army's procurement budget: if the Army's

---

3. CBO was unable to develop an independent estimate of the cost of a brigade's worth of equipment because some of the individual FCS components are not yet fully defined.

4. Statement of Paul L. Francis, Director, Acquisition and Sourcing Management, Government Accountability Office, before the Subcommittee on AirLand of the Senate Committee on Armed Services, published as Government Accountability Office, *Defense Acquisitions: Future Combat Systems—Challenges and Prospects for Success*, GAO-05-442T (March 16, 2005).

5. A fully mature technology, according to GAO's definition, is one that has been demonstrated in a prototype in an operational environment. In contrast, the Army considers a system that has been demonstrated in a prototype in a relevant environment to be sufficiently mature to be used in the SDD phase. The April 2005 independent assessment (Office of the Deputy Assistant Secretary of the Army for Research and Technology, *Technology Readiness Assessment Update*) was cited in Government Accountability Office, *Defense Acquisitions: Improved Business Case Is Needed for Future Combat System's Successful Outcome*, GAO-06-367 (March 2006).

procurement funding grew after 2011 at a rate equal to inflation—that is, if it remained at the same level in 2006 dollars—the FCS program's share of the service's planned $21 billion procurement budget would rise from almost 6 percent in 2011 to roughly 50 percent in 2015 and remain at or above 40 percent through 2025. (For comparison, the Army's purchase of ground combat vehicles during the 1980s peaked at 20 percent of the Army's total procurement budget.) Dedicating such a large proportion of the service's procurement funding to the FCS program would leave little money for purchasing other weapon systems (such as helicopters) or needed support equipment (such as generators and ammunition).

Also giving rise to experts' concerns is the fact that the FCS program has already experienced significant cost growth since it entered the SDD phase in spring 2003. At that time, the program's total acquisition cost for 15 brigades' worth of equipment—that is, including research, development, testing, evaluation, and procurement—was projected to be about $80 billion. The Army's latest estimate of that cost has increased to almost $130 billion, or roughly 60 percent more than its original estimate.[6] And if the history of the Army's major weapons programs is any indication, the costs of the FCS program may continue to rise. Historical trends suggest that DoD's major programs experience growth in R&D costs ranging from 16 percent to slightly more than 70 percent and growth in procurement costs ranging from 11 percent to roughly 70 percent—as measured from estimates prepared when the programs entered the SDD phase. (The higher end of the range reflects historical cost growth for ground vehicles.)

Overall, the different types of equipment that the FCS program plans to develop lead CBO to estimate that the Army's acquisition costs may grow by about 60 percent. Given some defense experts' view that the program's entry into the SDD phase was premature, the FCS program may continue to experience cost growth at historical rates. If it does, the average annual funding needed for

---

6. An independent estimate of the cost of the FCS program by the Cost Analysis Improvement Group (CAIG) in the Office of the Secretary of Defense was submitted to the Congress in June 2006 and suggests that the FCS program's costs may be higher than the Army's latest projections indicate. According to the CAIG, total acquisition costs for the FCS program, including costs for R&D and procurement, could range from $160 billion to $173 billion (in 2006 dollars).

the program, CBO estimates, may climb from the $8 billion to $10 billion projected most recently by the Army to between $13 billion and $16 billion.

Age of the Army's Armored Combat Vehicle Fleet

The total size of the FCS program—in terms of number of brigades' worth of equipment purchased—and the rate at which the program is executed will determine how many of the armored vehicles in the Army's current inventory must be retained and for how long. At the end of 2005, the Army had an armored combat vehicle fleet of almost 28,000 vehicles, including 5,850 Abrams tanks, 6,650 Bradley fighting vehicles, 13,700 vehicles based on the M113 personnel carrier, and 1,500 M109 self-propelled howitzers. Those vehicles, and the armored combat fleet as a whole, are aging. M113-based vehicles, which constitute almost half of the fleet, were first introduced into Army units in the 1960s. Most of the rest of the service's armored vehicles—namely, the Abrams tanks and Bradley fighting vehicles—are based on technology that is roughly 20 years newer. But at the end of 2005, even those vehicles, which have undergone several upgrades since they were first produced, had average ages of 15 and 11 years, respectively. Many of the vehicles that provide much of the Army's current combat power could thus reach the end of their useful service (based on a useful service life of 20 to 30 years) in the next decade—unless DoD invests significant sums in upgrading or modifying them.

The Army is currently reorganizing its fighting forces under what is known as its modularity initiative. That reorganization will reduce both the size of armored units and their total number; consequently, the service will need fewer armored vehicles and could retire more than 13,000 of its oldest by 2011. Those retirements would yield an armored vehicle fleet with a lower average age in that year than would have been possible without the extensive retirements. Nevertheless, the resultant fleet, with an average age of 13 years, would still be relatively old.

Although the FCS program could ultimately replace most of the armored vehicles that currently equip the Army's combat brigades, the average age of those vehicles before they were retired would significantly exceed the Army's guidelines. Manned FCS vehicles would not begin to be introduced into units until December 2014 at the earliest. By the time the Army began to field significant numbers of them—roughly 500 per year starting in 2018—the average age of the armored combat vehicle fleet would

Summary Figure 2.

Effect of the Administration's Plan for the FCS Program and Alternatives on the Average Age of the Army's Active Armored Combat Vehicle Fleet

(Average age in years)

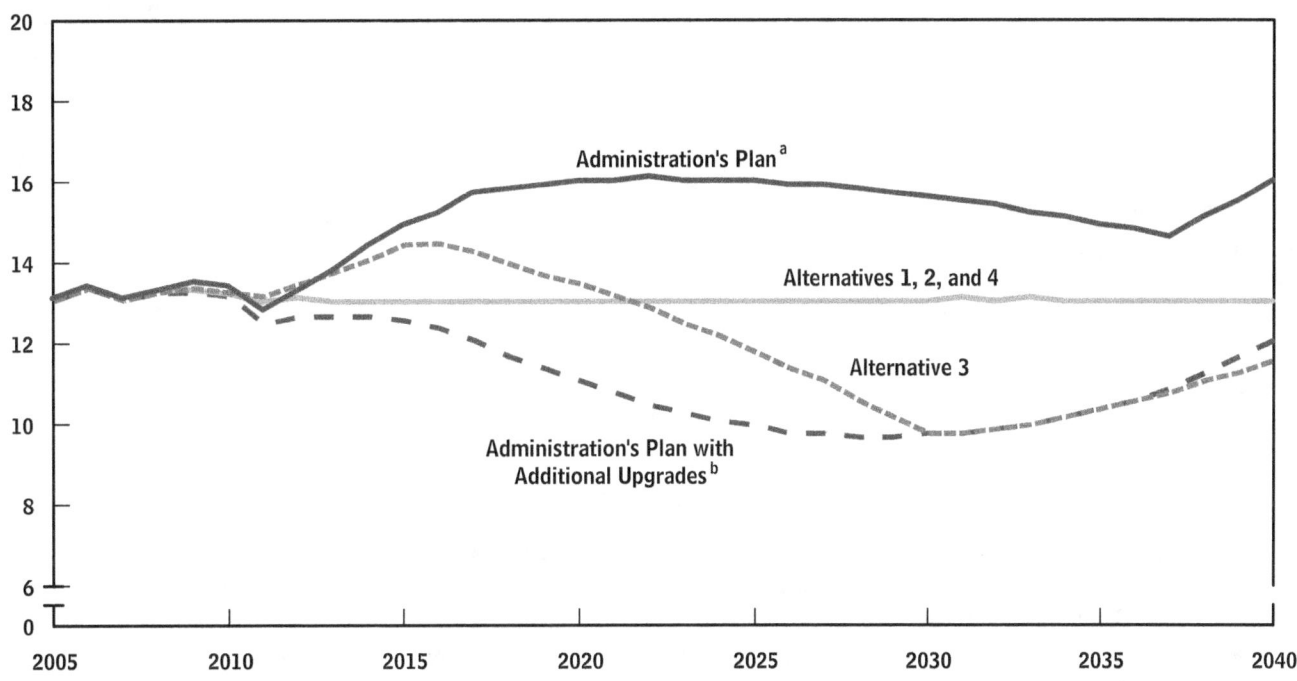

Source: Congressional Budget Office.

Notes: See Summary Table 4 for details of the alternatives.

The "active fleet" comprises all models of the vehicles that CBO estimates will be needed to equip and support modular units in both the Army's active component and the Army National Guard. (Modular units are those resulting from the Army's ongoing modularity initiative, which seeks to make the service more flexible by changing its structure from one based on 18 divisions, several of unique design, to one based on 70 combat brigades, each one of only three designs.)

FCS = Future Combat Systems.

a. Based on documents submitted with the President's 2007 budget, which includes $6 billion for upgrades to existing systems.

b. Includes upgrades to Abrams tanks, Bradley fighting vehicles, M113-based vehicles, and M109 howitzers to maintain a relatively constant average age for each fleet of vehicles after 2011.

be 16 years (see Summary Figure 2). Because the proposed annual purchases of armored vehicles under the FCS program represent only 3 percent of the total fleet, they will not begin to lower the fleet's average age until 2024—and even then, the average age could exceed 15 years (the high end of what the Army considers the desirable range) for the foreseeable future. If the Army continued to purchase manned FCS vehicles after the first 15 brigades' worth had been bought, armored vehicles in the combat brigades and prepositioned sets (brigade-sized sets of equipment that DoD has positioned and maintains in several locations around the world) would have been totally replaced by FCS vehicles by 2037.[7] Until

then, however, the Army's current fleet of armored vehicles would need to be maintained in fighting condition.

The Army aims to keep the average age of its armored vehicles at or below half of their useful life by, first, continually upgrading them to reflect the capabilities of the latest models and, second, incorporating FCS technologies into them as the new systems become available. To that end, documents submitted with the President's 2007

---

7. Some M113-based vehicles and self-propelled howitzers that equip units other than combat brigades could be retained indefinitely.

Summary Table 2.

Comparing the Army's Modular Heavy Combat Brigades and Brigades Equipped with Future Combat Systems

	Modular Heavy Combat Brigade[a]	FCS-Equipped Brigade
Personnel (Number)	3,800	3,300
Vehicles (Number)[b]		
Tracked[c]	370	320
Trucks, trailers, and other[d]	1,310	910
Total vehicles	**1,680**	**1,230**
Weight, All Equipment (Tons)	25,000	18,700
Coverage, All Equipment (Thousands of square feet)	320	260 to 290
Deployment of Equipment		
By air (Number of C-17 sorties)[e]	420	340 to 370
By sea (Number of ships)[f]		
Fast sealift	3	2
Large medium-speed roll-on/roll-off	2	1

Source: Congressional Budget Office based on data from the Department of the Army; Military Traffic Management Command Transportation Engineering Agency, *Deployment Planning Guide: Transportation Assets Required for Deployment*, MTMCTEA Pamphlet 700-5 (May 2001); and Department of the Air Force, *Air Mobility Planning Factors*, Pamphlet 10-1403 (December 18, 2003).

a.   "Modular" refers to the Army's ongoing modularity initiative, which seeks to make the service more flexible by changing its structure from one based on 18 divisions, several of unique design, to one based on 70 combat brigades, each one of only three designs. "Heavy" units are those equipped with tracked armored vehicles.

b.   Numbers are rounded to the nearest 10 vehicles.

c.   Includes all tracked armored vehicles.

d.   "Other vehicles" include wheeled vehicles that cannot drive for long distances on roads and the 20 helicopters and 150 unmanned ground vehicles in the FCS-equipped brigade.

e.   Based on an average load of 60 tons for modular heavy brigades and 50 tons to 55 tons for FCS-equipped brigades and rounded to the nearest 10 sorties.

f.   Either fast sealift ships or large medium-speed roll-on/roll-off ships will be needed but not both. Numbers of ships are rounded up to the nearest whole ship.

budget included roughly $6 billion from 2007 through 2016 for upgrades to Abrams tanks, Bradley fighting vehicles, and M113-based vehicles. To continue those upgrades, pay for modernization of the Army's M109 howitzers, and keep the average age of the vehicles required to equip its heavy units relatively constant after 2011, the Army must invest an additional $17 billion by 2025, in CBO's estimation.[8] That investment could bring the average age of the Army's fleet of combat vehicles down from one that without upgrades would exceed 16 years in 2020 to one that would remain consistently below 13 years (see Summary Figure 2).

Deployment of Army Units

Although a major goal of the FCS program is to make units equipped with armored vehicles easier to deploy overseas, replacing the Army's existing armored vehicles with FCS components will not significantly reduce deployment time. An FCS-equipped force would yield at most a 19 percent reduction in the time needed to deploy

---

8.   In developing that estimate, CBO assumed that in addition to incorporating systems that provided new capabilities, including some of those associated with the FCS network, an upgrade to an existing vehicle would also replace all components (such as engines and transmissions) needed to reset the vehicle's effective age to zero.

Summary Table 3.

Time Needed to Deploy Equipment of Combat Units to East Africa

(Days)

	Airlift[a]	Sealift
Brigade-Sized Units		
Administration's Plan[b]		
Modular heavy brigade with existing armored vehicles[c]	23	25
FCS-equipped brigade	18-20	25
Alternatives		
1. Information collection and sharing	23	25
2. Long-range strikes	24	25
3. New vehicular technology	24	25
4. Existing-system upgrades	23	25
Division-Sized Units[d]		
Administration's Plan[b]		
Four modular heavy brigades with existing armored vehicles[c]	135	27
Four FCS-equipped brigades	115-130	27
Alternatives		
1. Information collection and sharing	140	27
2. Long-range strikes	140	27
3. New vehicular technology	145	27
4. Existing-system upgrades	135	27

Source: Congressional Budget Office based on data from the Department of the Army; Military Traffic Management Command Transportation Engineering Agency, *Deployment Planning Guide: Transportation Assets Required for Deployment*, MTMCTEA Pamphlet 700-5 (May 2001); and Department of the Air Force, *Air Mobility Planning Factors*, Pamphlet 10-1403 (December 18, 2003).

Notes: Units would be moved from the continental United States. The data do not reflect the time needed to move sustaining units or supplies. See the text for more discussion of alternatives.

a. The number of daily sorties constrained by the capacity of the airfield in East Africa, based on average airlift payloads per brigade of 60 tons for modular heavy units and 50 tons to 55 tons for units equipped with Future Combat Systems.

b. Based on documents submitted with the President's 2007 budget.

c. "Modular" refers to the Army's ongoing modularity initiative, which seeks to make the service more flexible by changing its structure from one based on 18 divisions, several of unique design, to one based on 70 combat brigades, each one of only three designs. "Heavy" units are those equipped with tracked armored vehicles.

d. Besides combat brigades, divisions include headquarters and other support units.

heavy brigades by air. Whether equipped with current or FCS components, the Army's heavy units comprise hundreds of tracked (mostly armored) vehicles and hundreds more trucks and trailers that require multiple aircraft sorties to deploy by air (see Summary Table 2). Yet the lack of extensive paved surfaces for receiving and unloading aircraft at most airfields in the world (excluding large U.S. military facilities such as those in Germany) limits the number of daily sorties those airfields can support. CBO estimates that given those constraints, transporting a brigade equipped with the Army's existing armored vehicles to the east coast of Africa by air may take 23 days; moving an entire division similarly equipped may take 135 days, or more than four months (see Summary Table 3).[9] Brigades and divisions that are equipped with FCS components would take 18 to 20 days and 115 to 130 days, respectively.

In contrast, seagoing ships can easily transport very large amounts of the Army's existing equipment. Indeed, two or three of the Military Sealift Command's (MSC's) large seagoing ships can transport an entire brigade's worth of equipment, and eight of those vessels can transport an entire division overseas. Most coastal regions of the world have at least one large port capable of receiving the MSC's ships. And even though some of the equipment associated with a division equipped with either current armored vehicles or FCS components might have to be loaded onto some of the command's slower ships, it would still take far less time to deliver a full heavy division by sea—27 days—than by air.

Survivability

Finally, several observers have questioned the basic assumption that underlies the survivability of the lightweight FCS components—which is that those lightly armored vehicles will be able to survive on the battlefield because they will have extensive knowledge of the enemy's whereabouts, allowing them to avoid unexpected or disadvantageous encounters with enemy forces. If, however, the FCS sensors and communications network do not work as planned, the ability to avoid such encounters—and thus the armored vehicles' survivability—are uncertain. Moreover, other people, including soldiers returning from duty in Iraq, have argued that the most sophisticated sensors will not be able to detect and predict the kinds of dangerous situations that are now prevalent there.

9. CBO used as an example the transporting of Army units from the United States to Djibouti, on the east coast of Africa, to illustrate the trade-offs involved in moving units overseas.

Alternative Approaches to Modernizing the Army's Heavy Forces

CBO has analyzed four different options for modernizing the Army's armored units that would address major concerns about the FCS program—specifically, its technical feasibility, its cost, and the slow rate of introduction of its systems into the Army's force structure. Under the first three of those alternatives, the Army would retain different components of the FCS program (to emphasize systems that would contribute to different objectives of modernization) while canceling the remainder.

- Under Alternative 1, the Army would develop and purchase the full suite of sensors called for in the FCS program (to provide enhanced information-collection capabilities) and a version of the FCS network (to disseminate that information). With greater knowledge about the location and character of potential threats and the whereabouts of allies, Army forces, some argue, would be better able to respond and act appropriately, either individually or in concert.

- Under Alternative 2, in addition to developing and purchasing a scaled-down version of the FCS network, the Army would emphasize those of the program's systems that would enhance its ability to attack targets at ranges of greater than 20 km (that is, long-range strike missions).

- Under Alternative 3, the service would focus, first, on enhancing the maneuvering ability of the Army's combat brigades by developing several of the new manned ground vehicles (particularly those that would replace the older M113-based vehicles and M109 howitzers currently in the fleet) and, second, on developing and purchasing a modified version of the FCS network to tie them together.

- Under Alternative 4, the Army would greatly reduce the scope of the FCS program, developing only a scaled-down network and integrating it with existing systems.

Under none of the alternatives would the service develop or procure the unmanned ground vehicles or intelligent munitions systems that are currently planned for the FCS program; however, under all of them, it would upgrade existing armored vehicles to convert them to the latest model of the current system and prevent their average age from increasing. Such upgrades would also integrate the capabilities associated with the retained portions of the FCS program when those new systems became available (see Summary Table 4).

Alternative 1. Develop and Procure FCS Components That Will Collect and Disseminate Information

To collect as much information as possible, the Army under this alternative would develop and procure the unattended ground sensors and all four classes of unmanned aerial vehicles included in the FCS program. It would also develop a less ambitious and less extensive version of the FCS network and install it in existing armored vehicles so that they could receive and exchange the information collected by the FCS sensors. All other FCS components, including the manned and unmanned ground vehicles, the non-line-of-sight launch system, and the intelligent munitions system, would be canceled.

CBO estimates that total costs under this alternative—without taking historical cost growth into account—would be $99 billion from 2007 through 2025, versus $140 billion for the full FCS program (without upgrades) for the same period. (However, costs for this alternative could reach $131 billion if they grew as they have in the past for similar defense programs; under the Administration's plan for the FCS program through 2025, costs could grow to $231 billion.) Costs for the FCS components developed and purchased under this alternative would be $61 billion from 2007 through 2025, in CBO's estimation; costs for upgrading the existing armored vehicle fleet would be $38 billion for the same period (see Summary Table 5). Annual costs to implement Alternative 1, which are just under $6 billion after 2015, would include about $2 billion to upgrade roughly 560 vehicles per year (see Summary Figure 1 on page xiv).

One of the advantages of this approach is that the Army could introduce new technology into its units more rapidly than under the Administration's plan and at a lower cost. Because the service would be pursuing some of the least technologically risky of the FCS components, it could begin introducing them in 2010. And because those systems are also the least expensive of the 18 new components, the Army would purchase them at rates

Summary Table 4.

Emphasis of and FCS Components Included in Alternatives

Alternative	Emphasis	FCS Components	
		Retained	Canceled
Alternative 1	Collection and sharing of information	Scaled-down network All classes of UAVs Unattended ground sensors	All manned vehicles All unmanned ground vehicles Non-line-of-sight launch system Intelligent munitions system
Alternative 2	Long-range strikes	Scaled-down network UAV Classes III and IV Unattended ground sensors Non-line-of-sight launch system	All manned vehicles UAV Classes I and II All unmanned ground vehicles Intelligent munitions system

Alternative 3	New vehicular technology	Scaled-down network
		Manned vehicles
		   Medical
		   Infantry carrier[a]
		   Non-line-of-sight mortar
		   Non-line-of-sight cannon
		   Command and control
			All unmanned ground vehicles
			Manned vehicles
			   Mounted combat system
			   Recovery and maintenance
			   Reconnaissance and surveillance
			All classes of UAVs
			Non-line-of-sight launch system
			Unattended ground sensors
			Intelligent munitions system

Alternative 4	Network integration with existing systems	Scaled-down network	All manned vehicles All unmanned ground vehicles All classes of UAVs Unattended ground sensors Non-line-of-sight launch system Intelligent munitions system

Source: Congressional Budget Office.

Note: UAV = unmanned aerial vehicle; FCS = Future Combat Systems.

a.   Under Alternative 3, the Army would buy roughly 25 percent of the infantry carrier vehicles included in the Administration's plan.

twice as high as the Administration's planned 1.5 brigades' worth per year—that is, it would purchase 33 brigades' worth of the FCS sensors and UAVs as well as the network by 2025. And, CBO estimates, besides the lower total costs that this alternative would provide, relative to those under the Administration's plan, cost growth would probably also be less—30 percent compared with roughly 60 percent under the Administration's plan. Although the Army under this alternative would incorporate some of the capabilities for sharing information to be provided by the FCS network, vehicle survivability would not depend as heavily on those capabilities as it would under the Administration's plan.

The speed of deployment of the Army's heavy units would be little affected under this alternative because the service would retain the armored vehicles now in those units. Indeed, if the alternative was implemented, the weight of a typical heavy brigade would increase slightly —because additional trucks would be needed to support and transport the large number of UAVs that would be added to each brigade, increasing the time needed to airlift the brigade overseas by half a day. If transported by sea, however, the additional vehicles would not affect the time required to deploy a brigade- or division-sized unit—because the additional vehicles and supporting gear would fit easily on the ships used to move similar units with existing equipment (see Summary Table 3 on page xix).

Summary Table 5.

Total Acquisition Costs from 2007 to 2025 for the Administration's Plan and Alternatives

(Billions of 2006 dollars)

	Research and Development	Procurement	Total Acquisition
	Administration's Plan		
Costs Included in the President's Budget			
FCS Program's Increment 1[a]	21	101	122
Upgrades to existing vehicles	0	6	6
Further Costs as Estimated by CBO			
Continued purchases of FCS components, 2023 to 2025	0	18	18
Additional upgrades to existing vehicles[b]	2	15	17
Total	**23**	**139**	**162**
	Alternative 1. Collection and Sharing of Information		
FCS Components[c]	15	46	61
Upgrades to Current Systems[b]	2	36	38
Total	**17**	**82**	**99**
	Alternative 2. Long-Range Strikes		
FCS Components[d]	15	52	67
Upgrades to Current Systems[b]	2	36	38
Total	**17**	**89**	**106**
	Alternative 3. New Vehicular Technology		
FCS Components[e]	16	52	67
Upgrades to Current Systems[b]	2	33	35
Total	**18**	**85**	**103**
	Alternative 4. Existing-System Upgrades		
FCS Network	14	16	30
Upgrades to Current Systems[b]	2	36	38
Total	**16**	**52**	**68**

Source: Congressional Budget Office based on data from the Department of the Army.

Note: The estimated costs presented in this table do not take into account the possibility that costs may grow as they have in similar defense programs in the past.

FCS = Future Combat Systems.

a.   Includes costs to develop and purchase the first 15 brigades' worth of FCS components—enough to equip slightly more than half of the Army's planned 27 heavy brigades (19 brigades in the active Army and eight brigades in the Army National Guard).

b.   Includes upgrades to Abrams tanks, Bradley fighting vehicles, M113-based vehicles, and M109 howitzers to maintain a relatively constant average age for each fleet of vehicles after 2011.

c.   Includes unattended ground sensors, unmanned aerial vehicles (Classes I, II, III, and IV), and the network.

d.   Includes unattended ground sensors, unmanned aerial vehicles (Classes III and IV), the non-line-of-sight launch system, and the network.

e.   Includes manned vehicles (command and control, medical, non-line-of-sight mortar, non-line-of-sight cannon, and infantry carrier) and the network.

This alternative would suffer from several disadvantages when compared with the Administration's plan for the FCS program. Under this approach, the Army would retain the armored combat vehicles in its current fleet indefinitely, and by 2040, some of those vehicles would have been in the Army's inventory for almost 60 years. Another disadvantage is the technical risk involved in introducing network technology and associated communications links into old weapon systems, such as the Abrams tanks and Bradley fighting vehicles. Previous attempts to upgrade the communications and other electronic suites in those vehicles have met with difficulties.

Alternative 2. Develop and Procure FCS Components That Will Enhance the Army's Long-Range Strike Capability

Under the second alternative, the Army would retain those portions of the FCS program that enhanced its ability to carry out long-range strikes. Specifically, it would develop and procure the unattended ground sensors and longer-range UAVs (Classes III and IV) to detect and track targets. It would also develop and procure the non-line-of-sight launch system and its associated missiles to attack those targets. The combination of the UAVs and the missiles developed for the launch system would allow a brigade equipped with those weapons to identify and attack targets as far away as 70 km—long before most enemy weapons would be able to strike the corresponding U.S. targets. All of the ground vehicles in the FCS program, both manned and unmanned, would be canceled under this alternative, as would the shorter-range UAVs (Classes I and II) and the intelligent munitions system (see Summary Table 4 on page xxi). In addition, the Army would retain and upgrade the armored vehicles in its current inventory and develop and procure a scaled-down version of the FCS network (to tie the sensors and manned systems together).

Like the previous option, Alternative 2 would encompass the development and procurement of some of the least expensive of the proposed FCS components. As a result, annual procurement rates could be higher than under the Administration's plan, and annual savings—relative to that plan—could still be achieved. Specifically, the Army under this alternative would buy three brigades' worth of sensors, missile launchers, and network hardware annually starting in 2016 and continuing through 2025. Total costs for those systems, CBO estimates, would be $67 billion from 2007 through 2025 (see Summary Table 5).

Costs for upgrading the armored vehicles in the Army's current fleet would be identical to those under the previous alternative—$38 billion—over that same period.

All told, costs under this alternative would total $106 billion from 2007 through 2025—$7 billion more than the costs under Alternative 1 but considerably less than those under the Administration's plan. Annual costs under this alternative would be roughly $6 billion to $7 billion (see Summary Figure 1 on page xiv).

Compared with the Administration's plan, this alternative would increase the firepower of Army brigades sooner and at a lower cost. Because parts of the FCS program—primarily the high-risk ground vehicles—would be canceled, costs under this alternative would be $40 billion less from 2007 through 2025 compared with costs for the Administration's plan when it includes the full FCS program (but no upgrades), extended through 2025. Notwithstanding, high-volume missile launchers would be introduced into a larger proportion (almost two-thirds) of Army combat brigades. The potential for cost growth under Alternative 2 is also more favorable than under the Administration's plan—34 percent versus 60 percent. (If costs grew as they have in the past, acquisition costs under this alternative could be as high as $142 billion, compared with $231 billion for the full FCS program and planned upgrades.) Because the Army would invest significantly in upgrades under this approach, the average age of the resulting armored combat vehicle fleet would be much lower than that resulting under the Administration's plan (see Summary Figure 2 on page xvii). In addition, this alternative would achieve survivability by means other than dependence on what could be a problematic network.

In emphasizing systems that would improve the Army's ability to carry out long-range strikes, this alternative would not compare favorably with the Administration's plan on at least two counts. First, the Army would indefinitely retain armored vehicles that were originally designed in the 1970s or earlier, which could make it difficult to integrate those vehicles into a network that would tie them and the FCS sensors and launchers together. Second, under this alternative, the Army would increase the weight and bulk of its heavy units as trucks to support the UAVs and missile launchers from the FCS program were added to each brigade. As with the previous alternative, that would mean an increase—in this case, one day—in the time needed to deploy a heavy brigade by air but no increase in the time required to deploy it by sea (see Summary Table 3 on page xix).

Alternative 3. Emphasize Investment in New Manned Combat Vehicles

The third alternative envisions that the Army will develop and procure five types of manned vehicles through the FCS program to replace the oldest of its combat vehicles—the M113-based vehicles and M109 howitzers—currently assigned to combat brigades (see Summary Table 4 on page xxi). The FCS components would address at least some of the problems—such as the inability of the M109 howitzers to keep up with the newer models of the Abrams tank and Bradley fighting vehicle—that the Army has said are associated with keeping the older vehicles in its combat units. The Army's other armored vehicles (the Abrams tanks and Bradley fighting vehicles and those M113-based vehicles and M109 howitzers in units outside of heavy combat brigades) would be retained and upgraded so that they could be integrated into a scaled-down FCS network, which is another element of this alternative. All other parts of the FCS program—specifically, all four classes of UAVs, all unmanned ground vehicles, the non-line-of-sight launch system, the unattended ground sensors, the intelligent munitions system, and the remaining three types of manned FCS vehicles—would be canceled (see Summary Table 4 on page xxi).

CBO estimates that costs under this alternative will be similar to those under the previous two alternatives, requiring a total investment (excluding cost growth) of $103 billion from 2007 through 2025. Of that total, $67 billion would be needed to develop the five variants of manned vehicles and purchase 23 brigades' worth of equipment by 2025. Upgrading the armored vehicles retained under this alternative would cost $35 billion from 2007 through 2025 (see Summary Table 5 on page xxii).

Because the manned vehicles are among the most technically challenging of the FCS components and require the longest time to develop, purchases of those systems under this alternative would not begin until 2014. Consequently, the annual funding required would be less than that required under the previous two alternatives and the Administration's plan—until 2015 (see Summary Figure 1 on page xiv). Furthermore, because manned vehicles represent the most expensive of the 18 FCS components, their annual purchases would be limited to two brigades' worth, one fewer than under the previous two alternatives. Nevertheless, annual costs for this option, at

roughly $6.5 billion, would be slightly greater than those under the previous two alternatives after 2015 but still significantly less than those under the Administration's plan.

Among the approaches CBO considered, this alternative is unique in its introduction of new vehicular technology into the Army's forces. Because new armored combat vehicles would be introduced more quickly under this alternative than under any other—including the Administration's plan—some of the Army's oldest armored vehicles would be retired earlier, and the average age of the resulting fleet would ultimately be the lowest (see Summary Figure 2 on page xvii). The alternative's costs are on a par with those of Alternatives 1 and 2; they are less than those of the Administration's plan. But because this alternative would emphasize the development and procurement of ground vehicles, which have experienced the highest rate of historical cost growth, the potential for such a rise in costs is greater—at 55 percent—than under the previous two alternatives and could add $57 billion to total costs.

This alternative shares some disadvantages with Alternatives 1 and 2. Under this approach, the Army would indefinitely retain both the Abrams tank and Bradley fighting vehicle fleets—whose original designs date from more than 30 years ago—and would attempt to incorporate the technology associated with the FCS network into those vehicles, a plan that could pose technical difficulties. Moreover, implementing the alternative would have little effect on units' deployment. On average, FCS vehicles would replace about half of the armored vehicles now in a heavy brigade; roughly 90 percent of those existing vehicles would be M113-based systems—which weigh less than the FCS vehicles that would replace them. As a result, the total weight of a heavy brigade could increase by as much as 6 percent under this alternative and in turn add one day to the time it would take to deploy such a brigade overseas by air. However, the time required to deploy either a brigade- or division-sized unit by sea would not increase (see Summary Table 3 on page xix).

Alternative 4. Develop a Scaled-Down FCS Network and Integrate It with Existing Systems

The last alternative that CBO examined would preserve only that portion of the FCS program designed to develop and support the network (see Summary Table 4 on page xxi). The new capability—a scaled-down version of the network currently envisioned for the FCS program—would then be incorporated into existing armored vehicles, allowing the Army's combat brigades to benefit from an evolutionary improvement rather than a wholesale makeover based on unproven technology. All other portions of the FCS program would be canceled.

Under Alternative 4, the Army would purchase the least amount of hardware, by comparison with that purchased under the other alternatives, and would incur the lowest costs—$68 billion from 2007 through 2025. CBO estimates that $30 billion of that total will be needed to develop and purchase the hardware for the FCS network and that costs to upgrade the Army's existing armored vehicles will be $38 billion (see Summary Table 5 on page xxii). Some of the capabilities of the FCS network would be incorporated into the Army's current fleet of vehicles under this alternative, but the survivability of those vehicles would not be at risk if the network failed to perform as planned. Despite the fact that three brigades' worth of FCS network hardware would be purchased annually starting in 2012, the annual funding needed to implement this alternative would be roughly $3 billion in 2018 and thereafter (see Summary Figure 1 on page xiv). Under this alternative, the Army would have purchased enough network hardware by 2025 to upgrade almost two-thirds of its combat brigades. Moreover, because the Army would not develop or purchase any FCS components with high historical rates of cost growth, the potential for such growth under Alternative 4 would be relatively low—about 40 percent, or a total additional cost of $26 billion.

The speed of deployment of Army units overseas would be unaffected under this alternative because no new weapon systems would be added to existing Army combat brigades and no existing systems would be replaced by new ones. The time needed to deploy a heavy brigade overseas by air or by sea would be the same as it is for brigades equipped with existing armored vehicles—23 days and 25 days, respectively. Similarly, there would be no change in the time needed to deploy a division-sized unit by sea, which would remain at 27 days (see Summary Table 3 on page xix).

Because this alternative calls for so little investment in new technologies and equipment, it would also offer the fewest benefits from innovation, relative to the other approaches. Even though upgrades would maintain the average age of the Army's fleet of armored vehicles at about 13 years through 2040 and the vehicles would be connected by a new network, they would still be the same systems that the Army has had for the past 20 years. And some of them—notably those based on the M113 chassis—have been in the Army's armored combat vehicle fleet since the Korean War.

The Army's Heavy Forces and Armored Vehicles

The Army has long maintained a sizable force equipped with armored vehicles that were seen as particularly necessary during the Cold War to deter or defeat the extensive armored forces of the Soviet Union. (Units equipped with armored vehicles are referred to as "heavy" units; the rest of the Army's combat forces are referred to as "light" units.) Since the fall of the Berlin Wall, some analysts have questioned the military relevance of armored forces; nevertheless, heavy units figured prominently in the opening days of ground combat in both Operation Desert Storm and Operation Iraqi Freedom. And they continue to be useful in other types of operations, such as the ongoing military activities in Iraq.

At the end of 2003, before the Army began its current reorganization initiative, the service maintained a fleet of more than 30,000 armored vehicles to equip and support the heavy units that made up roughly 50 percent of its combat forces. Almost half of those vehicles had been bought between 1980 and 1990 as part of the substantial investment in weapons known as the Reagan defense buildup; the remainder were first introduced in the 1960s. Thus, the original design of the Army's armored vehicles is decades old, although all of them have been upgraded and overhauled at least once since they were first placed in service.

Despite that ongoing modernization, which in many instances produces what is essentially a new vehicle, the average age of the Army's current armored combat vehicle fleet is relatively high, and the status of that fleet has prompted concerns among the Army's leadership. Perhaps most pressing is the fact that the weight and size of some armored vehicles prohibit them from being easily transported by air. For all practical purposes, heavy combat units (divisions and brigades or, before the Army's reorganization, brigade combat teams) must be transported overseas by ship, a process that takes weeks.[1] In an era of rapidly evolving conflicts, the Army wants forces that have the combat power of heavy units but that can be transported anywhere in the world in a matter of days.

To address those concerns, the Army has undertaken two initiatives. The first—called modularity—would reorganize all of the Army's combat forces into smaller, more standardized units. That process, when completed, will allow the service to reduce the overall size of its armored fleet and retire some of its older armored vehicles. The second initiative, the Future Combat Systems (FCS) program, is a major modernization effort designed in part to develop and purchase a total of 18 new weapon systems, including eight manned vehicles, to replace most of the armored systems now used in heavy units. The new vehicles would be much lighter than many of those the Army has now, which would make units equipped with them easier to deploy.

But the Army's plans for the FCS program raise additional issues. The new FCS vehicles would be lighter, but they would also be more expensive—because of the sophisticated communications gear, sensors, and active protection devices that would replace the extra weight of armor to ensure the vehicles' survivability. Because of the cost, the Army plans to buy fewer than 500 manned FCS vehicles each year starting in 2015 at the earliest. Consequently, some of the vehicles now in the Army's heavy units will be kept in the force for at least 30 more years—long after the end of their useful service life.

Adding to concerns that the FCS program raises about retaining already aging vehicles for extended periods are

---

1. A heavy brigade combat team included between 3,000 and 5,000 soldiers, roughly 300 armored vehicles, and various support units. In 2003, the Army put together such teams for specific operations; they are currently being replaced by heavy modular units. (See the discussion in Chapter 2.) Also in 2003, a heavy division, with roughly 15,000 soldiers, typically included three brigade combat teams and additional support units.

Figure 1-1.

The Army's Armored Combat Vehicle Fleet, 1980 to 2003

(Thousands of vehicles)

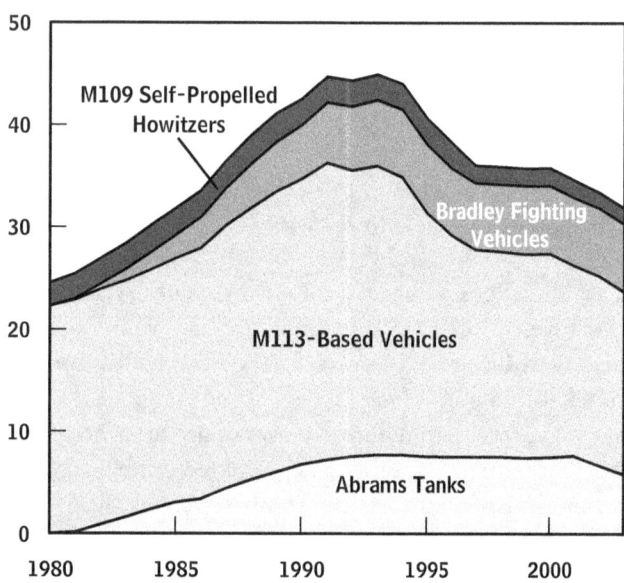

Source: Congressional Budget Office based on data from the Department of the Army.

questions about the initiative's technical feasibility and affordability. Some experts, including the Government Accountability Office (GAO), doubt whether the Army can develop and test the technologies necessary to start producing lightweight manned vehicles by 2012—the schedule that must be met to begin fielding the vehicles in December 2014, as the Army now plans.[2] (The fielding date has slipped seven years since the program was initiated in 2000.) Another concern is the availability of funds to purchase FCS components in the quantities currently envisioned—1.5 brigades' worth of equipment annually (which represents a reduction from the Army's original plan of three brigades' worth). The Army plans a force structure that includes a total of 27 heavy brigades; any further drop in the FCS procurement rate will force the

service to retain its current fleet of armored vehicles longer and to invest more funds in maintaining and upgrading it.

This Congressional Budget Office (CBO) study examines the Army's FCS program and the concerns it has generated. The report considers the status of the Army's fleet of armored vehicles in 2003 and in the future and assesses the ease of deployment of the Army's heavy forces. In addition, it describes the FCS program; explores its costs, advantages, and disadvantages; and compares it with several alternative plans for modernizing the Army's heavy forces.

Overview of the Army's Armored Vehicle Fleet at the End of 2003

The Army's armored combat vehicle fleet—composed primarily of tanks, fighting vehicles, personnel carriers, and self-propelled howitzers—has shrunk since 1995, but at the end of 2003, it still included almost 32,000 vehicles of various types (see Figure 1-1). Almost all of them have been modernized since they were first produced; nevertheless, in 2003, several thousand of them were 18 years old or older. Furthermore, at the end of 2003, the average age of the fleet was roughly 12 years, which exceeds the Army's preferred level.[3]

Types of Vehicles in the Fleet
Armored combat vehicles are designed to protect soldiers as they attack the enemy, move about the battlefield, perform scouting or reconnaissance missions, or transport ammunition and other cargo to forces in hostile environments. The armored vehicle fleet mainly comprises just a few types of vehicles: those noted above (specifically, the Abrams tank, the Bradley fighting vehicle, the M113 armored personnel carrier, and the M109 self-propelled howitzer) and multiple-rocket launchers. Except for the rocket launchers, those types of armored vehicles are all found in the Army's combat brigades; the service expects

---

2. Statement of Paul L. Francis, Director, Acquisition and Sourcing Management, Government Accountability Office, before the Subcommittee on AirLand of the Senate Committee on Armed Services, published as Government Accountability Office, *Defense Acquisitions: Future Combat Systems—Challenges and Prospects for Success*, GAO-05-442T (March 16, 2005); and Government Accountability Office, *Defense Acquisitions: Improved Business Case Is Needed for Future Combat System's Successful Outcome*, GAO-06-367 (March 2006).

3. The Department of Defense aims to maintain the average age of its fleets of aircraft and vehicles at or below half of their useful life span. (For a discussion of desired fleet age, see Congressional Budget Office, *The Long-Term Implications of Current Defense Plans*, January 2003.) At various times, the Army has defined the useful life of its armored vehicles as 20 or 30 years, yielding desired half-lives of 10 or 15 years. The Army's preference is to prevent the average age of the fleet from exceeding 10 years.

Table 1-1.

Characteristics of Models of the M1 Abrams Tank in 2003

	Model		
	IP	A1	A2
Date of Introduction	1985	1985	1991
Combat Weight (Tons)	61	67	70
Size of Main Gun (Millimeters)	105	120	120
Improvements Over Previous Model			
Armor	Improved composite armor	n.a.	Second-generation depleted-uranium armor
Other	n.a.	Improved suspension Active NBC protective system	Commander's independent thermal viewer Digital electronics
Status of Fleet in 2003			
Number of vehicles	764	4,294	790
Average age (Years)	17	14	3

Source: Congressional Budget Office based on its February 1993 report *Alternatives for the U.S. Tank Industrial Base* and Gary W. Cooke, "Gary's Combat Vehicle Reference Guide," available at www.inetres.com/gp/military/cv/index.html.

Note: IP = Improved; n.a. = not applicable; NBC = nuclear, biological, and chemical.

to replace those systems with variants of the manned vehicles being developed as part of the FCS program.

Abrams (M1) Tank. This weapon system was developed in the 1970s, during the height of the Cold War, when defeat of the Soviet Union's armored forces was of premier importance. During the 1980s and 1990s, the tank's design underwent changes intended to enable it to attack targets from greater distances or to penetrate thicker armor. Subsequent modifications have generally included improved and heavier armor for greater protection and improved electronic and communications equipment (see Table 1-1 and Figure 1-2).[4] The latest version of the tank weighs more than 70 tons and is so large and heavy that the Air Force's newest cargo aircraft, the C-17, can carry only one Abrams tank at a time; the largest transport aircraft in the U.S. fleet, the C-5, can carry only two. At the end of 2003, the Army's Abrams tank fleet was a mix of three models with an average age of roughly 13 years and totaling approximately 5,850 vehicles.

Bradley Fighting Vehicle. Developed at the same time as the Abrams tank, the Bradley fighting vehicle was designed to replace at least some of the service's older M113

armored personnel carriers. The Bradley is equipped with a 25-millimeter (mm) gun; tube-launched, optically tracked, wire-guided (TOW) antitank missiles; and a 7.62-mm machine gun (see Figure 1-3).[5] The design of the vehicle has undergone many changes since it was introduced in 1981, including an improved version of the TOW missile system and enhanced protection of the crew and passengers (see Table 1-2 on page 6). The Army has produced very few new Bradley fighting vehicles since 1995, but upgrades to existing vehicles have yielded a fleet with an average age of 10 years in 2003—which is considerably lower than the original production dates of 1980 to 1994 would indicate. Even though the Bradley fighting vehicle weighs less than one-half as much as an Abrams tank, it, too, can be airlifted only by a C-17 or a C-5 and has been most commonly transported overseas by ship.

M113-Based Vehicles. The Army began developing the original M113 in 1956 as a lightweight multipurpose

---

4.   Appendix A describes in more detail the various models of the Abrams tank and of the Army's other armored vehicles.

5.   The Bradley fighting vehicle has been produced in two variants, but the differences between them are minor. Because of the kind of missions it undertakes, the M3 cavalry fighting vehicle carries more radios and missile rounds than does the M2 infantry fighting vehicle, which can carry more soldiers (in addition to the crew of three, six versus two for the M3).

Figure 1-2.

Abrams Tank

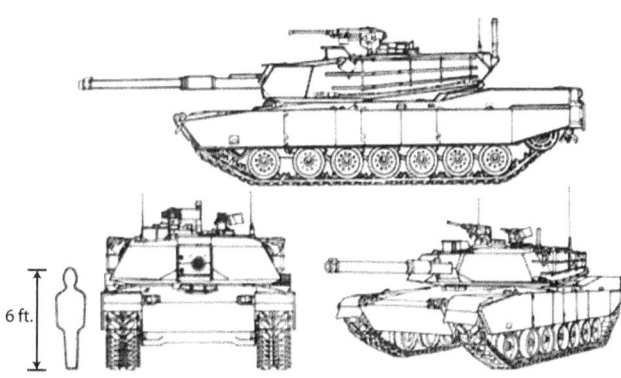

6 ft.

Source: Gary W. Cooke, "Gary's Combat Vehicle Reference Guide,"
available at www.inetres.com/gp/military/cv/index.html.

personnel carrier (see Figure 1-4). Since then it has fielded the vehicle in several versions, including as a smoke generator, mortar carrier, cargo carrier, command post, antitank-missile carrier, and personnel carrier. The most numerous of the Army's armored vehicles, with roughly 18,000 in service at the end of 2003, the M113 is also the Army's only armored vehicle that weighs less than 20 tons—which makes it considerably lighter than either the Abrams tank or the Bradley fighting vehicle. Since it was first introduced, the M113 vehicle has been modified several times—for example, by switching the vehicle's engine from gasoline to diesel fuel, improving its suspension and transmission, and adding an antispall liner (to protect occupants and equipment from hull fragments; see Table 1-3 on page 7). Although the Army has produced no new M113s since 1992, it has continued to convert older models to newer configurations—with the result that the average age of the M113 fleet at the end of 2003 was only slightly greater than 13 years.

M109 Self-Propelled Howitzer. The howitzer, part of the Army's inventory since 1963, provides supporting fire for the Army's combat units; its 155-mm cannon can shell targets at distances of up to 30 kilometers (km), or approximately 20 miles (see Figure 1-5 on page 8). Weighing roughly 30 tons, the howitzer is the largest of the Army's current fleet of armored vehicles and has been modified several times, but only the most recent upgrade represented a significant change. That conversion of older howitzers to the A6, or Paladin, configuration added supplemental armor and an antispall liner, enhanced the ve-

hicle's suspension and its hydraulic and electrical systems, and installed a new fire-control computer (see Table 1-4 on page 9). Those extensive modifications, combined with the decommissioning of many older models in the mid-1990s, resulted in an average age for the howitzer fleet at the end of 2003 of 11 years.

Armored Combat Vehicles in the Army's Current Force Structure

The armored vehicles described above are found primarily in the Army's combat divisions and brigades. At the end of 2003, those units were more heavily represented in the Army National Guard than in the Army's active component (see Table 1-5 on page 10).[6] At that time, six of the active component's 10 divisions and seven of the National Guard's eight divisions were equipped with armored vehicles. Other units so equipped included one armored cavalry regiment (ACR) in the Army's active component and seven separate brigades and one ACR in the National Guard.

The Army had more than enough armored vehicles in its fleet at the end of 2003 to fully equip its heavy units—even if some of those vehicles were relatively old. The surplus was primarily due to the reduction in forces in the early 1990s, when the Army eliminated about one-third of its force structure and personnel but retained many of the vehicles it had purchased in the 1980s to equip a much larger force. The service's total requirements for armored vehicles, however, encompass more than those needed to equip units in the force structure. Vehicles are also needed at various locations for training soldiers in their use and maintenance and for replacing vehicles that are removed from units for repairs or upgrades or that are lost in accidents or in combat. The factors that the Army uses for its planning indicate a range of 13 percent to 20 percent of the total number of vehicles in units as the number of additional vehicles needed for training and replacements.[7] In its estimates of the number of additional

---

6. The Army announced early in calendar year 2004 that it would reorganize its forces into so-called modular units. The discussion in this chapter describes the premodular Army—that is, before the reorganization. Chapter 2 describes modularity and its implications for the armored vehicle fleet.

7. Colonel Larry Hollingsworth, "Combat Systems—Where We Are . . . Where We're Going. . . " (presentation to the National Defense Industrial Association, Combat Vehicle Conference, Fort Knox, Ky., September 20–22, 2005).

Figure 1-3.

Bradley Fighting Vehicle

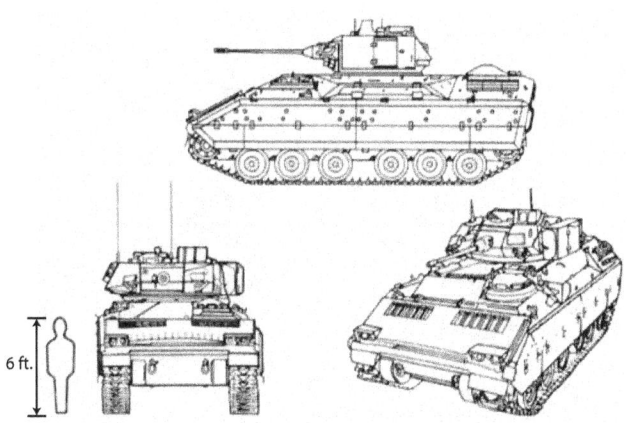

6 ft.

Source: Gary W. Cooke, "Gary's Combat Vehicle Reference Guide,"
          available at www.inetres.com/gp/military/cv/index.html.

vehicles required to equip and support the Army's units, CBO used an assumption of 15 percent.

In addition, the Army maintains sets of equipment for heavy units in various places around the world, allowing soldiers to fly from their home station—generally in the United States—and collect their equipment at locations overseas. That policy of prepositioning equipment was first used in Central Europe, where the Army maintained six divisions' worth in case of a major Soviet attack on Western Europe. Since the end of the Cold War, most of those stocks have been retired or redistributed to form several smaller sets of equipment located around the world. Before Operation Iraqi Freedom, equipment for five combat brigades was stored in South Korea, the Middle East, Europe, and onboard ships, adding to the overall inventory of equipment required for the Army's heavy units (see Table 1-6 on page 12).

To equip, maintain, and support the heavy combat force that existed at the end of 2003, the Army needed roughly 4,650 Abrams tanks, 5,650 Bradley fighting vehicles, 11,650 M113-based vehicles, and 1,350 M109 self-propelled howitzers, CBO estimates. At that time, the service's inventories included roughly 5,850 tanks, 6,650 fighting vehicles, almost 18,000 M113-based vehicles, and about 1,500 howitzers—more than enough to equip and fully support its heavy forces.

Issues Regarding Today's Armored Forces and Vehicles

In recent years, defense officials and independent observers have voiced concerns about the Army's existing armored vehicles and its heavy units. Predominant among such issues are the vehicles' weight and their extensive support requirements (which make heavy units difficult to move overseas quickly) and the average age of the current armored combat vehicle fleet. Two other aspects of the current fleet also trouble Army leaders, factors that are linked to the continual upgrading and modernization that the vehicles have undergone since their introduction. One is that as the vehicles have been modified and improved, they have become heavier and less fuel efficient. The other is the mixture of models of each type of vehicle in the Army's fleets, which increases the burden of maintenance and training associated with them.

Heavy Vehicles and Units are Difficult to Deploy

In its official statements, the Army has stressed the importance of a quick response to crises anywhere in the world. As noted earlier, however, it is impractical, if not infeasible, to transport the Army's heavy units, with their hundreds of armored vehicles, by air. Consequently, when heavy units are deployed overseas, they are typically transported on ships, and because a transoceanic voyage takes several days, if not weeks, deployment by sea can be a lengthy process.

Figure 1-4.

M113 Armored Personnel Carrier

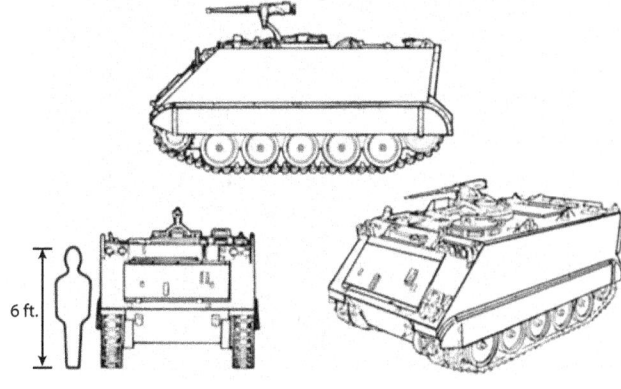

6 ft.

Source: Gary W. Cooke, "Gary's Combat Vehicle Reference Guide,"
          available at www.inetres.com/gp/military/cv/index.html.

Note: This is the vehicle that forms the basis for the M113 family of vehicles.

Table 1-2.

Characteristics of Models of the M2/M3 Bradley Fighting Vehicle in 2003

	Model		
	A0	A2[a]	A3
Date of Introduction	1981	1988	1999
Combat Weight (Tons)	25	32	33
Improvements Over Previous Model			
Armor	n.a.	Additional appliqué armor	Titanium roof armor
Other	n.a.	Digital communications Antispall liner[b] Improved TOW missile system NBC filter system	Second-generation FLIR for commander's independent viewer and driver's vision enhancer
Status of Fleet in 2003			
Number of vehicles	1,517	4,793	349
Average age (Years)	19	7	1

Source: Congressional Budget Office based on Gary W. Cooke, "Gary's Combat Vehicle Reference Guide," available at www.inetres.com/gp/ military/cv/index.html.

Note: n.a. = not applicable; FLIR = forward-looking infrared; TOW = tube-launched, optically tracked, wire-guided; NBC = nuclear, biological, and chemical.

a. Includes improvements and inventory for A2 Operation Desert Storm models.

b. The liner protects vehicle occupants from hull fragments.

Deploying Heavy and Light Army Units. The equipment found in the Army's heavy units and that found in its light units differs substantially, and that divergence allows light units to be more easily deployed. Not only do the Army's light divisions have no armored combat vehicles but they have roughly 50 percent fewer vehicles overall than heavy divisions have (see Table 1-7 on page 13). Moreover, at least two-thirds of the trucks in light divisions are high-mobility multipurpose wheeled vehicles (HMMWVs), the smallest of the Army's trucks. It is thus realistic to assume that a light division's equipment could be transported by air to remote airfields if the need arose.[8]

In contrast, heavy divisions, equipped with roughly twice as many vehicles as light divisions, are typically moved by sea. Their additional equipment primarily comprises hundreds of armored vehicles and heavy and medium-weight trucks (see Table 1-7 on page 13).[9] Furthermore, as noted earlier, most of the armored vehicles are so large and heavy that they must be transported not by the Air Force's large fleet of C-130 aircraft but by its less numerous but bigger C-17s or C-5s—aircraft that require bigger and better-prepared landing facilities. As a result, in many cases, moving even a heavy brigade combat team (roughly equivalent to one-third of a division) by air is impractical.

The time and the ships or aircraft required to transport Army units from the United States to Djibouti, a small nation on the coast of East Africa, illustrate why some Army leaders consider today's heavy units too cumber-

---

8. In fact, the 82nd Airborne Division and two light infantry divisions were designed for just such a contingency, and portions of the 82nd Airborne and the 10th Light Infantry divisions have been flown into Afghanistan to participate in operations there. In addition, a brigade of the 82nd Airborne Division is always on alert and ready to be airlifted to a crisis anywhere in the world.

9. Compared with an airborne division, an armored division has over a thousand more trucks but is equipped with roughly the same number of HMMWVs. The armored division's additional trucks include roughly 600 medium-sized trucks (each weighing 10 tons to 13 tons) and 350 heavy trucks (each weighing roughly 20 tons).

Table 1-3.

Characteristics of Models of M113-Based Vehicles in 2003

	Model	
	A2	**A3**
Date of Introduction	1979	1986
Combat Weight (Tons)	12	14
Improvements Over Previous Model		
Armor	Not applicable	Provisions for bolt-on armor
Other	Diesel engine Improved suspension	Antispall liner[a] Greater horsepower diesel engine Improved transmission Automotive-type steering and brake controls
Status of Fleet in 2003		
Number of vehicles	11,654	6,185
Average age (Years)	15	10

Source: Congressional Budget Office based on Gary W. Cooke, "Gary's Combat Vehicle Reference Guide," available at www.inetres.com/gp/
military/cv/index.html; and Christopher Foss, ed., *Jane's Armour and Artillery, 1979-1980* (New York: Wyatt Publishing, 1979).

a.   The liner protects vehicle occupants from hull fragments.

some. (Djibouti—7,700 miles from the East Coast of the United States—has strong military ties to the United States and according to the Central Intelligence Agency is "a frontline state in the global war on terrorism.")[10]

Deploying Forces to Djibouti by Air. In transporting a large amount of equipment to Djibouti by air, the Army faces certain constraints. Djibouti's transportation infrastructure is limited: for example, only three of its airports have paved runways. If those airports were extensive, with many taxiways and large aprons, the Air Force's planned fleet of 180 C-17s could support 65 sorties per day capable of delivering roughly 3,000 tons to 4,000 tons of equipment.[11] That level of capacity would mean that the Army could move light infantry or airborne brigade combat teams from the United States to Djibouti by air in only one or two days; it could move a light infantry division or an airborne division in roughly one week. Theoretically, even an armored brigade combat team could be moved in seven days (see Figure 1-7 on page 14).

10. See the entry on Djibouti in the Central Intelligence Agency's *The World Factbook*, available at www.cia.gov/cia/publications/factbook/index.html.

However, the type of facilities needed to handle the number of daily sorties required to deliver up to 4,000 tons of equipment are found only at very large airports, such as those at Ramstein Air Force Base in Germany. None of the airports in Djibouti is big enough to handle the number of aircraft that would be on the ground at one time if 65 C-17s were arriving and departing each day. In fact, most airports in places in which crises are likely to occur would have space for only a few C-17s unloading and being serviced at the same time. In that case, the number of daily C-17 sorties would be limited to fewer than 20, even with 24-hour operations, and the amount of equipment delivered to Djibouti in one day would be reduced to between 1,000 tons and 1,200 tons. At that rate, transporting an armored brigade combat team by air would

11. The range in the amount of equipment delivered by the same number of sorties reflects the fact that C-17s loaded with heavy equipment, such as tanks, can carry more tonnage per sortie than they can when transporting equipment from light units because the heavy vehicles that will fit in the aircraft weigh more. According to an analysis by the Department of Defense's Military Transportation Command, C-17s that transport equipment from heavy units carry an average of 60 tons per sortie; those that deliver equipment from light units have an average payload of 50 tons or less. (Appendix B describes how CBO estimated the time needed to move units overseas by air.)

Figure 1-5.

M109 Self-Propelled Howitzer

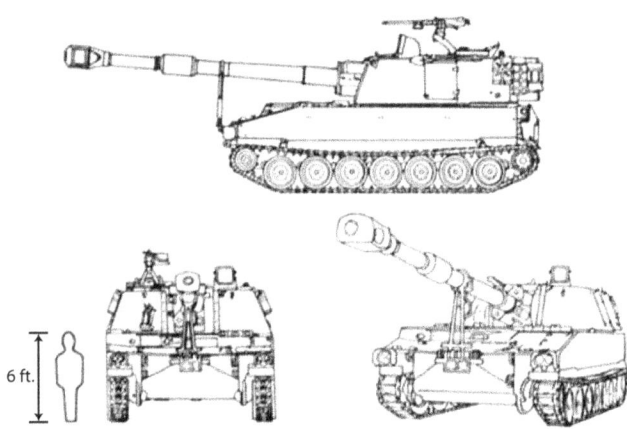

6 ft.

Source: Gary W. Cooke, "Gary's Combat Vehicle Reference Guide," available at www.inetres.com/gp/military/cv/index.html.

take 23 days. For sustained operations, total daily deliveries would be reduced to less than 800 tons, and it could take more than 100 days to deliver an armored division (see Figure 1-7 on page 14).[12]

Another critical factor is that those estimates of deployment times incorporate the assumption that the Air Force's entire C-17 fleet is devoted to ferrying the heavy units' equipment from the United States to Djibouti. In an actual conflict, the Air Force would have other responsibilities as well, including transporting equipment for its own needs, for large air-defense systems, and for other purposes (such as opening ports or handling materiel arriving at airfields). In past conflicts, the Army has received substantially less than 100 percent of the United States' airlift capacity to move equipment associated with its combat units.

Deploying Forces to Djibouti by Sea. Moving equipment by sea, particularly heavy and bulky equipment, is a viable and sometimes attractive alternative to moving it by air. Djibouti, for example, has one large port that can accommodate large seagoing vessels, including the fast sealift ships (FSSs) and large medium-speed roll-on/roll-off ships (LMSRs) operated by the Military Sealift Command (MSC) to transport U.S. forces overseas.[13] The estimated time such ships would require to deliver their cargo to Djibouti—which includes readying the ships, moving Army units from their home stations to a port such as Savannah, loading the ships, sailing to Djibouti, and unloading the ships—is 25 days (for FSSs) and 27 days (for LMSRs).[14]

The MSC's fleet of eight FSSs and 11 LMSRs is more than adequate to move any one of the Army's divisions in one sailing. In fact, the FSS fleet alone could move a light division or even a heavy brigade combat team. However, the equipment associated with a heavy division would require more capacity than could be provided by FSSs alone. Consequently, the time needed to deliver a full armored division would be two days longer than that required to deploy a light division—because of the slower speed of the LMSRs. All told, 25 days would be needed to deliver light units or a heavy brigade to Djibouti by sea, and 27 days would be required to deliver a heavy division (see Figure 1-7 on page 14).

Other Considerations. Another factor to take into account in estimating the time needed to deploy an Army unit overseas is that a division—and to a greater extent, a brigade—cannot operate for long in a theater (particularly an undeveloped one) without supporting units and supplies (including ammunition, fuel, food, water, and spare parts). Most units carry supplies for only a limited time—typically, three days for a brigade-sized unit. The air- or sealift capacity to bring in additional supplies and supporting units must be added to that required to deploy brigades and divisions themselves.

Heavy units need perhaps the most support of any of the Army's forces. Armored vehicles, such as the Abrams tank and Bradley fighting vehicle, have very low fuel efficiency (they can travel less than 2 miles on a gallon of fuel). Consequently, heavy units in combat burn fuel at a high

---

12. Expedited, or "surge," operations (usually 24 hours a day) are generally sustained for limited periods—typically, 45 days—during the early stages of a crisis. After that, the level of effort is reduced to one that can be maintained indefinitely.

13. The ships in the MSC's fleet can be ready in four days to be loaded with Army equipment. FSSs and LMSRs have average transit speeds of 27 knots and 24 knots, respectively.

14. CBO's estimates of the time required to deploy units overseas cover only the time needed to deliver the unit's equipment to an air- or seaport and not the time needed to reconstitute the unit or move it to a marshaling area away from the port. For a more detailed discussion of the assumptions and methods CBO uses to estimate deployment times by sea, see Congressional Budget Office, *Options for Strategic Military Transportation Systems* (September 2005), Chapter 2.

Table 1-4.

Characteristics of Models of the M109 Self-Propelled Howitzer in 2003

	Model	
	A2/A3/A4/A5	A6 (Paladin)
Date of Introduction	1962 [a]	1992
Combat Weight (Tons)	28	32
Size of Cannon (Millimeters)	155	155
Improvements Over Previous Model		
Armor	Not applicable	Supplemental armor
Other	Not applicable	Antispall liner[b]
		Onboard ballistic computer
		Improved suspension
		Enhanced engine cooling
		Driver's night-vision device
		Enhanced hydraulic and electrical systems
Status of Fleet in 2003		
Number of vehicles	542 [c]	975
Average age (Years)	19	6

Source: Congressional Budget Office based on Gary W. Cooke, "Gary's Combat Vehicle Reference Guide," available at www.inetres.com/gp/
           military/cv/index.html.

a.   Date of introduction of the original M109 howitzer.

b.   The liner protects vehicle occupants from hull fragments.

c.   Includes only A4 and A5 models.

rate—about 420,000 gallons of fuel per day for a heavy division, according to one source.[15] To meet such demands, each heavy division is equipped with about 170 tankers, each holding 2,500 gallons—and the tankers also need fuel to perform their mission. That small example of the logistics burden associated with heavy units illustrates why it is difficult to deploy and operate them without a large support structure—an area of concern to Army leaders.

The Armored Combat Vehicle Fleet Is Aging

More than half of the Army's armored combat vehicles are based on systems that were introduced in the 1960s, and even the most recent models are based on technology that is roughly 25 years old. Moreover, despite the upgrades that almost all the vehicles have undergone since they were first produced, some of the individual fleets at the end of 2003 contained large numbers of very old vehicles. Specifically:

- More than 2,500 of the 5,850 Abrams tanks had been in service 15 years or more, and 540 tanks had been in service 18 years;

- Of the roughly 6,650 Bradley fighting vehicles in the fleet, 370 were 20 years old, and more than 1,500 were at least 15 years old;

- More than half of the M113-based vehicles were produced or rebuilt at least 15 years ago, and almost 1,000 had been commissioned 18 years earlier; and

- Almost 300 of the M109 self-propelled howitzers were at least 20 years old.

The average age of the entire armored combat vehicle fleet at the end of 2003—12 years—exceeded the Army's preferred average age of 10 years. Furthermore, the average age of each of the individual fleets—except that of the howitzers—has been rising steadily since 1990 (see Figure 1-6). The useful service lives of armored

---

15. Bryant Jordan and Sean Naylor, "Too Heavy," *Army Times* (September 6, 1999), p. 14.

Table 1-5.

Army Units Equipped with Armored Vehicles in 2003

	Army's Active Component	Army National Guard	Total Army
	Divisions		
Armored and Mechanized Infantry	6	4	10
Infantry	0	3	3
Total	**6**	**7**	**13**
	Separate Brigades or Regiments		
Armored	0	3	3
Mechanized Infantry	0	4	4
Armored Cavalry	1	1	2
Total	**1**	**8**	**9**

Source: Congressional Budget Office based on Assistant Secretary of the Army for Financial Management and Comptroller, *The Army Budget: FY04/05 President's Budget* (February 2003).

vehicles may extend from 20 years to 30 years; however, unless the Army continues to invest significant amounts in upgrades or modifications, many of the vehicles that currently provide much of its combat power will reach the end of their useful lives in the next decade.

Armored Vehicles Are Getting Bigger and Heavier

The armored vehicles that make up the Army's current fleet have grown heavier and larger as the service has modified and improved them. With the addition of armor and more-sophisticated electronic gear, the weight of succeeding models of each of the four types of armored vehicles has increased significantly over that of the corresponding original model.

■ The weight of the Abrams tank has grown by more than 16 percent, rising from 60 tons when the basic version of the tank was introduced in 1981 to more than 70 tons for the latest model—which, in addition to more and heavier armor, is equipped with a larger main gun.

■ The most recent version of the Bradley fighting vehicle weighs 33 tons, almost one-third more than the original vehicle introduced in 1981, which weighed 25 tons.

■ The weight of the M113 armored personnel carrier has grown from its original 12 tons in 1961 to 14 tons for the latest model.

■ The M109 self-propelled howitzer has become 14 percent heavier—its weight rising from 28 tons to 32 tons—with the fielding of the latest model in 1992.

The increase in weight has led, in general, to a decrease in fuel efficiency, which intensifies the logistics burden of supporting these vehicles in combat or in other operations. Another concern of the Army's planners is that the latest model of the Abrams tank is too heavy for many bridges in Europe, particularly older ones. Moreover, both the Abrams tanks and the Bradley fighting vehicles are too wide (12 feet and 11 feet, respectively) for many roads in built-up areas. Thus, the size and weight of the Abrams tank in particular and, to a lesser extent, of the Bradley fighting vehicle limit the vehicles' usefulness in constricted spaces (such as urban environments) or in areas where roads and bridges are not designed to carry very heavy or very wide loads.

Figure 1-6.

Average Age of the Army's Armored Combat Vehicles, 1990 to 2003

(Average age in years)

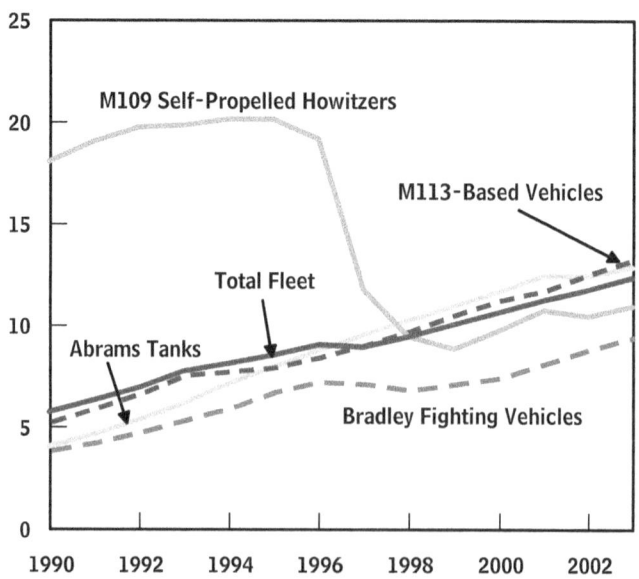

Source: Congressional Budget Office based on data from the Department of the Army.

Each Armored Vehicle Fleet Comprises Several Models

At the end of 2003, the Army's armored vehicle fleets contained several different models of each type of vehicle—three models for the Abrams tank and for the Bradley fighting vehicle and two for the M113 and for the M109 fleets.[16] Except in the case of the M109 howitzer, most of the vehicles in a given fleet at the end of 2003 were not the latest model.

■ The A1 model of the Abrams tank, introduced in 1985, accounted for almost three-quarters of the tank inventory; the latest model, the A2, accounted for only 14 percent.

■ Of the Bradley fighting vehicle fleet in 2003, the latest A3 model, introduced in 1999, represented only 5 percent of vehicles, whereas the A2 model, introduced in 1988, accounted for the vast majority of the rest.

■ The older A2 version of the Army's M113-based vehicles, introduced in 1979, accounted for roughly two-thirds of that fleet; the more modern A3 model accounted for the remainder.

■ In contrast, most—64 percent—of the fleet of M109 self-propelled howitzers were the updated A6 model introduced in 1992; the rest were older versions.

The reason that more of the Army's armored vehicles are not the latest model may be the expense involved in converting older models to the most modern version. Converting an A1 model of the Abrams tank to the A2 model, for example, costs roughly $5 million. Converting A2 models of the Bradley and M113-based vehicles to the A3 model of each costs $4 million and $400,000, respectively.

---

16. That enumeration ignores variants of specific models—for example, it treats the Abrams A1 and Abrams A1 AIM as one model.

Because the Army has not converted all of its armored vehicles to their most modern form, it cannot provide the same equipment to all of its heavy units. In 2003, the service did not have enough of its most modern Abrams tanks or Bradley fighting vehicles to equip all of the heavy units in the Army's active component—which in the past have received the latest versions of equipment before units in the National Guard (see Figure 1-8 on page 15). The mix of models in the vehicle fleets means that some active-component units will have the latest models of armored vehicles (A2 versions of the Abrams tank, A3 versions of the Bradley fighting vehicle, and A3 versions of the M113 personnel carrier); other active-component units will have a mix of various models; and many units in the National Guard will have the oldest models in the fleet.

The lack of uniformity among models of the vehicles that equip active-component units and National Guard units may cause problems in deployments and operations. Some units may deploy without their own equipment and either pick up prepositioned items or retrieve equipment left behind by units that preceded them. If either the prepositioned or retrieved equipment is different from the vehicles that units have trained on or are familiar with, problems may develop in the field. Furthermore, a mismatch of equipment between active-component and National Guard units may make it difficult for units from the two components to operate effectively together.

In 2003, for example, roughly one-third of the heavy units in the Army's active component were equipped with the A2 model of the Abrams tank, and the rest were equipped with the A1 version. In contrast, three-quarters of National Guard units were equipped with the A1 model, and the rest had an older version—the Abrams IP—whose main gun is a smaller caliber than the guns on the two other models of the tank. Moreover, the sets of equipment prepositioned in the Middle East and onboard ship were equipped with the A1 model of the tank. Thus, both the Army's active-component units and units from the National Guard might arrive in Iraq and be expected to use tanks with which they were not familiar.

Table 1-6.

Armored Vehicles Needed to Equip and Support the Army's Heavy Units in 2003

	Abrams Tanks	Bradley Fighting Vehicles	M113-Based Vehicles	M109 Self-Propelled Howitzers
	Number of Armored Vehicles per Unit[a]			
Divisions				
Armored or mechanized infantry	250	300	500	54
Infantry	150	200	350	36
Separate Brigades or Regiments				
Armored	100	60	190	18
Mechanized infantry	50	100	190	18
Armored cavalry	120	140	160	18
	All Armored Vehicles[b]			
Combat Brigades and Divisions				
Active component	1,600	1,950	3,150	350
National Guard	2,050	2,500	4,550	450
Other Units	0	0	1,500	300
Subtotal, vehicles in units	3,650	4,450	9,200	1,100
Prepositioned Equipment	450	550	1,050	100
Operational Readiness Float and Training Base[c]	550	650	1,400	150
Total	**4,650**	**5,650**	**11,650**	**1,350**

Source: Congressional Budget Office based on information from the Department of the Army's WebTAADS database (an Internet version of The Army Authorization Document System, or TAADS, maintained by the Army Force Management Support Agency's Requirements Division) and the Operating and Support Management Information System (OSMIS).

Note: "Heavy" units are those equipped with armored vehicles.

a. Requirements for Abrams tanks, Bradley fighting vehicles, and M113-based vehicles are rounded to the nearest 50 vehicles for divisions and to the nearest 10 vehicles for brigades and regiments.

b. Rounded to the nearest 50 vehicles.

c. Represents vehicles needed at various locations for training soldiers in their use and maintenance and for replacing vehicles that are removed from units for repairs or upgrades or that are lost in accidents or in combat.

Table 1-7.

Comparing the Army's Light Infantry, Airborne, and Armored Units in 2003

	Divisions			Brigade Combat Teams		
	Light Infantry	Airborne	Armored	Light Infantry	Airborne	Armored
Personnel (Number)	12,100	13,500	17,300	2,700	3,100	3,800
Vehicles (Number)						
Tracked[a]	10	10	1,560	0	0	450
Trucks	2,520	2,910	4,060	420	570	840
Towed	950	1,090	2,090	130	180	390
Other[b]	130	220	130	10	10	10
Total	3,610	4,230	7,840	560	760	1,690
Weight (Tons)						
All vehicles	13,600	14,700	83,000	2,300	2,700	21,100
Total for unit	19,200	25,400	99,900	2,900	4,200	25,000
Area Covered (Thousands of square feet)						
All vehicles	483	566	1,406	71	97	305
Total for unit	563	907	1,502	80	111	323
Deployment of Equipment						
Airlift (Number of C-17 sorties)[c]	425	530	1,720	60	90	420
Sealift (Number of ships)[d]						
Fast sealift ships	3.7	5.9	9.8	0.6	0.7	2.1
Large medium-speed roll-on/roll-off ships	2.0	3.2	5.4	0.3	0.4	1.2

Source: Congressional Budget Office based on data from the Department of the Army; and Military Traffic Management Command Transportation Engineering Agency, *Deployment Planning Guide: Transportation Assets Required for Deployment,* MTMCTEA Pamphlet 700-5 (May 2001).

a.   Includes all tracked armored vehicles.

b.   Includes helicopters and wheeled vehicles that cannot drive long distances on roadways.

c.   Based on a maximum allowable cabin load of 65 tons for a leg of 3,200 nautical miles and rounded to the nearest five sorties.

d.   Either fast sealift ships or large medium-speed roll-on/roll-off ships will be needed but not both.

Figure 1-7.

Time Needed to Deploy Equipment of Combat Units from the Continental United States to East Africa

(Days)

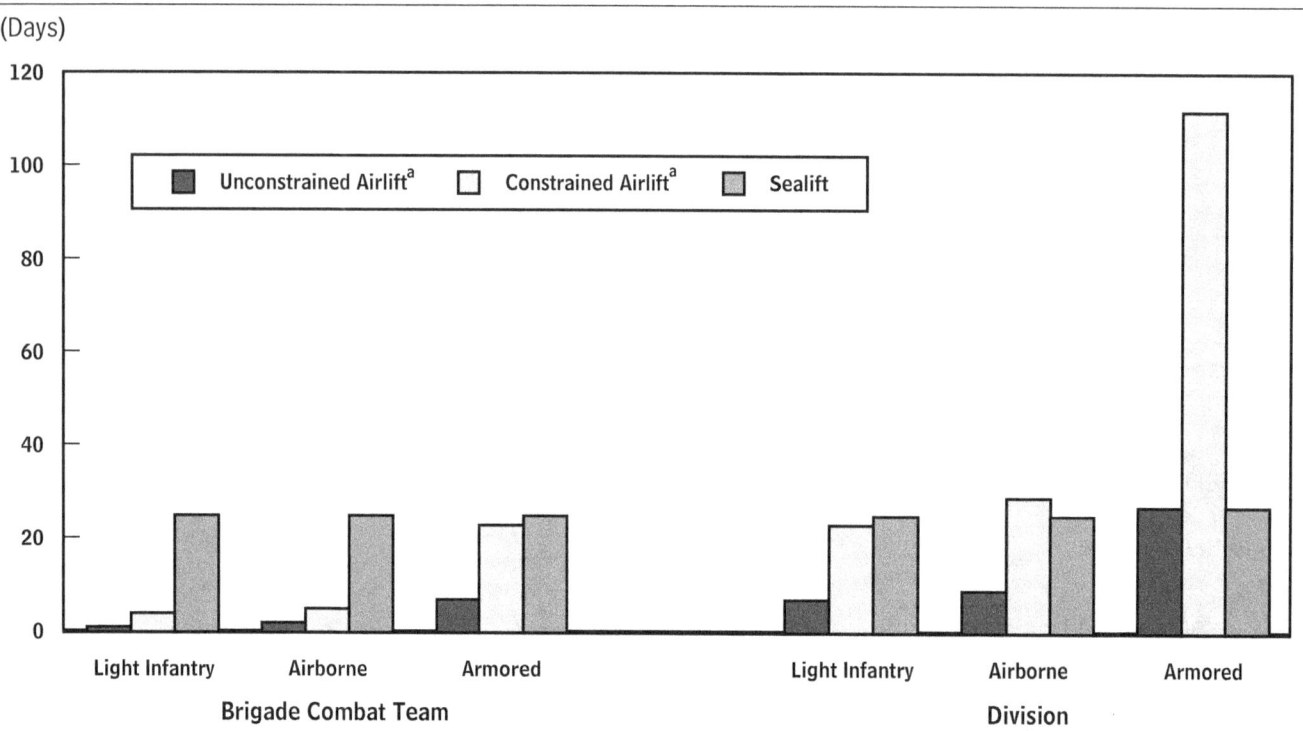

Source: Congressional Budget Office based on data from the Department of the Army; Military Traffic Management Command Transportation Engineering Agency, *Deployment Planning Guide: Transportation Assets Required for Deployment*, MTMCTEA Pamphlet 700-5 (May 2001); and Department of the Air Force, *Air Mobility Planning Factors*, Pamphlet 10-1403 (December 18, 2003).

Note: The data do not reflect the time needed to move sustaining units or supplies.

a.   "Unconstrained" and "constrained" refer to whether the number of daily sorties to deliver equipment is constrained (or not) by the airfield's capacity to accommodate aircraft and handle cargo.

Figure 1-8.

Requirements and Inventories for the Army's Armored Combat Vehicles in 2003

(Thousands of vehicles)

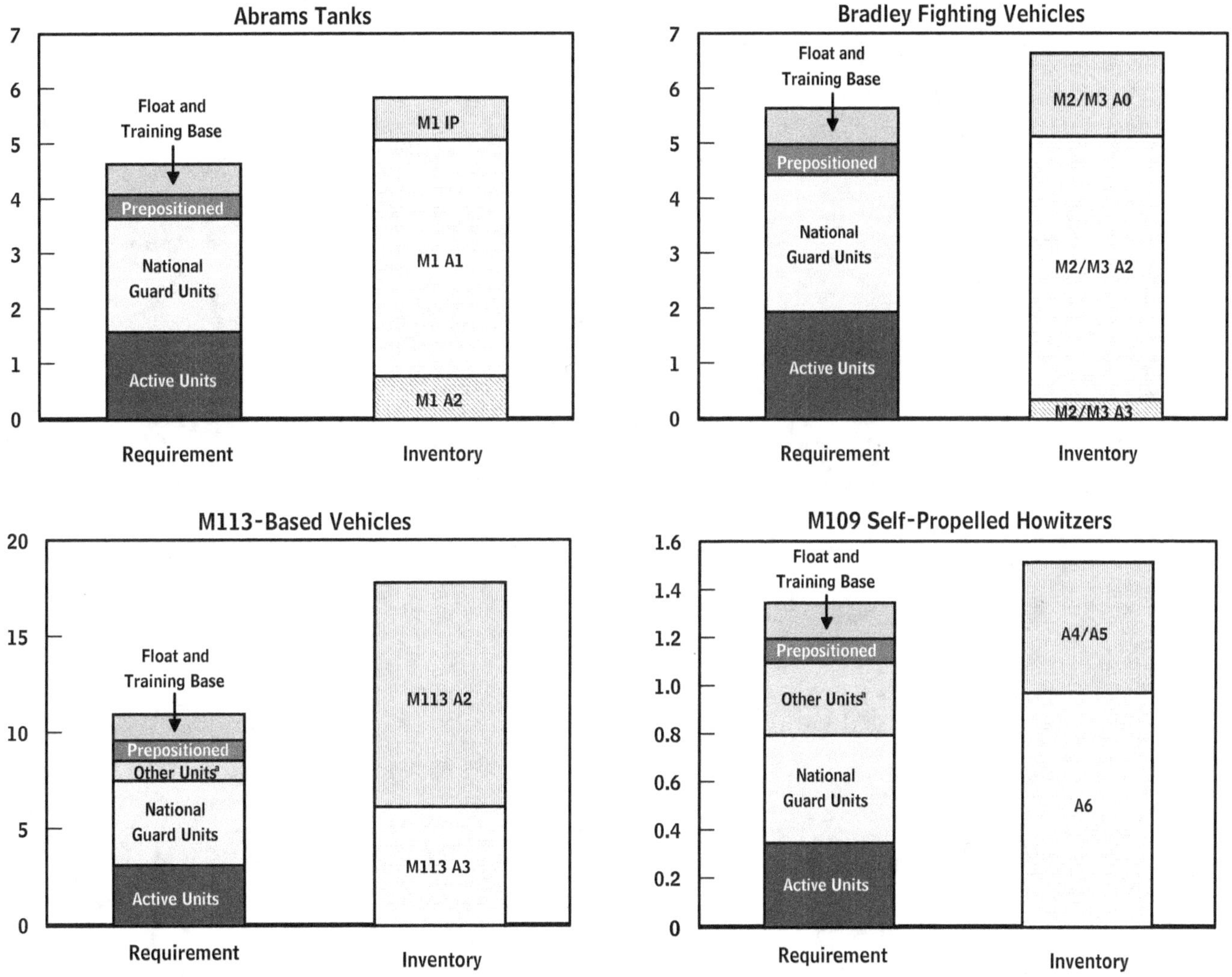

Abrams Tanks

Float and Training Base
Prepositioned
National Guard Units
Active Units
Requirement

M1 IP
M1 A1
M1 A2
Inventory

Bradley Fighting Vehicles

Float and Training Base
Prepositioned
National Guard Units
Active Units
Requirement

M2/M3 A0
M2/M3 A2
M2/M3 A3
Inventory

M113-Based Vehicles

Float and Training Base
Prepositioned
Other Units[a]
National Guard Units
Active Units
Requirement

M113 A2
M113 A3
Inventory

M109 Self-Propelled Howitzers

Float and Training Base
Prepositioned
Other Units[a]
National Guard Units
Active Units
Requirement

A4/A5
A6
Inventory

Source: Congressional Budget Office.

Note: The "float and training base" category represents vehicles needed at various locations for training soldiers in their use and maintenance and for replacing vehicles that are removed from units for repairs or upgrades or that are lost in accidents or in combat. The "prepositioned" category represents sets of equipment located at various sites around the world that allow quick deployment of units.

a.   Reflects vehicles in units outside of divisions and combat brigades.

Description of the Army's Modularity Initiative and Future Combat Systems Program

The changing global political environment has led the Army to undertake several initiatives that are designed to enable its forces to respond rapidly and capably to conflicts arising anywhere in the world. One of those plans, the modularity initiative, would reorganize the Army's fighting forces into smaller, more standardized units so that they could be used interchangeably and in whatever combination was best suited to a particular crisis. Another initiative, the Future Combat Systems program, would develop and field a total of 18 new systems as well as a communications network. The FCS components would include several new unmanned air and ground vehicles and replacements for the armored vehicles in the Army's current fleet (which were developed decades ago) featuring lighter platforms of entirely new design. The schedule for developing and fielding the FCS components has changed several times since the program began, and its ambitiousness together with the program's complexity have raised questions about the program's ultimate success.

The Modularity Initiative

In February 2004, the Army announced that it would restructure its combat forces to make them more agile and flexible. Until then, under the service's so-called premodular structure, most of its combat forces had been organized into divisions that typically comprised three combat—or maneuver—brigades in addition to several support components, such as engineer units, artillery units, and signal units.[1] At the end of 2003, the Army's combat forces included 10 divisions in the active compo-

nent and eight divisions in the Army National Guard as well as several combat brigades and regiments outside those divisions.

That force structure, however, has not been well suited to some recent military operations. For example, once the situation in Bosnia and Kosovo had been stabilized and troops of the North Atlantic Treaty Organization had gained control, U.S. peacekeeping operations there required less than a full division's worth of combat forces. As a result, one or two combat brigades from a division would be deployed, along with the division headquarters and other support units, for what would typically be a six-month rotation. After that, another brigade or two, often from a different division, would replace them. The Army found such reconfigurations of parts of divisions into smaller packages, or task forces, to be disruptive.

To create what Army Chief of Staff General Peter Schoomaker described in February 2004 as a more responsive and more easily deployable force, the service began restructuring its organization from one based on 18 divisions, several of unique design, to one based on 70 combat brigades, each one of only three designs. The Army also expects to restructure and standardize its division and corps headquarters units and the support units that had been assigned to the divisions and corps within its premodular force structure.

Comparing the Army's Modular and Premodular Force Structures

The Army's modularity initiative, if carried out as planned, will touch almost all aspects of its force structure. Although the service's active component will retain its 10 division headquarters under the reorganization, it

---

1. An exception to that structure was the 10th Mountain Division, which had only two combat brigades in 2003.

Table 2-1.

Comparing the Army's Premodular and Modular Combat Force Structures

	Active Component	Army National Guard	Total Army
Premodular Brigades, End of 2003			
Heavy[a]	18	23	41
Light[b]	12	15	27
Stryker[c]	3	0	3
Total	**33**	**38**	**71**
Modular Brigades Planned for 2011			
Heavy	19	8	27
Infantry	17	19	36
Stryker[c]	6	1	7
Total	**42**	**28**	**70**

Source: Congressional Budget Office based on data from the Department of the Army and a private Army briefing, "The Army Modular Force, 2004–2020" (July 2005).

Note: "Premodular" and "modular" refer to the Army's ongoing modularity initiative, which seeks to make the service more flexible by changing its structure from one based on 18 divisions, several of unique design, to one based on 70 combat brigades, each one of only three designs.

a.   Includes armored cavalry regiments and armored and mechanized infantry brigades.

b.   Includes light infantry, infantry, airborne, and air assault brigades as well as scout units.

c.   Brigades that are equipped with medium-weight Stryker wheeled armored vehicles.

will alter the units associated with them.[2] Divisions, which in the premodular Army were typically assigned three combat brigades, will have four such units associated with them in the modular Army. And combat brigades, which in the premodular Army comprised only combat units (such as infantry battalions and tank battalions), will now include some support units as well (such as artillery units and engineer units). In that way, the Army argues, each modular combat brigade will be more self-contained and able to operate more effectively on its own.

Modular combat brigades are designed to be the basic unit for carrying out the Army's missions.[3] Most of the Army's armored vehicles will be found in such brigades, and it is there that the new FCS vehicles will ultimately be assigned. Thus, the remainder of this discussion of the Army's modularity initiative will focus on changes in its

combat brigades and in particular on those brigades that contain armored vehicles.

Number of Heavy Brigades. As planned in early calendar year 2006, the Army will field fewer heavy brigades under its modular structure than under its premodular organization. At the end of 2003, the service had 41 heavy brigades—18 active-component units and 23 National Guard units (see Table 2-1). The Army is planning to

---

2.   The Army plans to reduce the number of division headquarters in the National Guard from the current eight to six by 2011.

3.   Under the modularity initiative, division support units will be organized into brigades (aviation, artillery, and support) that closely parallel those found in premodular divisions. Support units outside of divisions will also be organized into brigades (combat aviation; fires; combat support maneuver enhancement; battlefield surveillance; and sustainment). For a more complete discussion of the changes resulting from the Army's initiative, see U.S. Army Training and Doctrine Command, *Army Comprehensive Guide to Modularity*, vol. 1, version 1.0 (October 8, 2004); Congressional Budget Office, *Options for Restructuring the Army* (May 2005); and Andrew Feickert, *U.S. Army's Modular Redesign: Issues for Congress*, CRS Report for Congress RL32476 (Congressional Research Service, May 5, 2006).

Table 2-2.

Comparing the Army's Premodular Heavy Brigade Combat Teams and Modular Heavy Combat Brigades

	Premodular Brigade Combat Teams		Modular Heavy Brigade
	Mechanized Infantry	Armored	
Personnel	4,000	3,800	3,800
Vehicles			
Tracked[a]			
Abrams tanks	55	95	60
Bradley fighting vehicles	110	65	120
M113-based vehicles	190	190	120
M109 self-propelled howitzers	20	20	15
Other	75	80	50
Subtotal, tracked vehicles	450	450	365
Trucks[b]	810	840	880
Towed[b]	390	390	410
Other[c]	10	10	20
Total	**1,660**	**1,690**	**1,675**

Source: Congressional Budget Office based on data from the Department of the Army; Military Traffic Management Command Transportation Engineering Agency, *Deployment Planning Guide: Transportation Assets Required for Deployment*, MTMCTEA Pamphlet 700-5 (May 2001); Department of the Army, Cost and Economic Analysis Center, FORCES Cost Model, Version 2003.0513; and Colonel Larry Hollingsworth, "Combat Systems—Where We Are . . . Where We're Going. . . " (presentation to the National Defense Industrial Association, Combat Vehicle Conference, Fort Knox, Ky., September 20–22, 2005).

Note: "Premodular" and "modular" refer to the Army's ongoing modularity initiative, which seeks to make the service more flexible by changing its structure from one based on 18 divisions, several of unique design, to one based on 70 combat brigades, each one of only three designs.

a. Rounded to the nearest five vehicles.

b. Rounded to the nearest 10 vehicles.

c. Includes wheeled vehicles that cannot drive for long distances on roads.

increase—from 33 to 42—the total number of combat brigades (of all types) in its active component. Of those 42, 19 will be heavy brigades—one more than the number fielded under the premodular structure. At the same time, the service expects to reduce the number of combat brigades in the National Guard to 28 (according to its plans in March 2006), or 10 fewer than at the end of 2003—a reduction that would come mostly at the expense of the Guard's heavy units. Consequently, by 2011, with the reorganization complete and all units converted to the modular design, the Army would have 27 heavy combat brigades—14 fewer than it had in 2003. Furthermore, the Army's active component in 2011 would have more heavy combat brigades than the National Guard would have, reversing the situation that prevailed at the end of 2003.

Brigade Design and Size. Under the premodular force structure, heavy combat brigades that were part of a division typically included about 2,000 soldiers. When engaged in an operation, a brigade would typically be augmented by artillery, engineer, cavalry, and other support units, creating what the Army terms a brigade combat team. With those additional units, a premodular heavy brigade combat team (one with armored or mechanized infantry units) would typically include about 4,000 soldiers (see Table 2-2).

A heavy combat brigade under the modular structure will have roughly the same number of soldiers but fewer "combat" units: only two combined arms battalions compared with the three combat battalions (tank or mechanized infantry) that are typically part of a premodular

Table 2-3.

Armored Combat Vehicles Needed to Equip and Support the Army's Modular Heavy Combat Brigades in 2011

	Abrams Tanks	Bradley Fighting Vehicles	M113-Based Vehicles	M109 Self-Propelled Howitzers
Heavy Brigades[a]				
Active component (19 brigades)	1,100	2,300	2,300	300
National Guard (Eight brigades)	450	950	950	150
Subtotal	1,550	3,250	3,250	450
Other Units[b]	0	0	2,300	200
Prepositioned[c]	300	600	600	100
Operational Readiness Float and Training Base[d]	400	650	650	150
Total	**2,250**	**4,500**	**6,800**	**900**
Memorandum:				
Total Vehicles Required for the Premodular Army in 2003	4,650	5,650	11,650	1,350
Total Vehicles in Inventory as of 2005	5,850	6,650	13,700	1,500

Sources: Congressional Budget Office based on data from the Department of the Army's WebTAADS database (an Internet version of The Army Authorization Document System, or TAADS, maintained by the Army Force Management Support Agency's Requirements Division); U.S. Army Ground Combat Systems Program Executive Office, *Fleet Management Strategy* (June 2005); and Colonel Larry Hollingsworth, "Combat Systems—Where We Are . . . Where We're Going. . . " (presentation to the National Defense Industrial Association, Combat Vehicle Conference, Fort Knox, Ky., September 20–22, 2005).

Notes: Numbers are rounded to the nearest 50 vehicles.

"Premodular" and "modular" refer to the Army's ongoing modularity initiative, which seeks to make the service more flexible by changing its structure from one based on 18 divisions, several of unique design, to one based on 70 combat brigades, each one of only three designs.

a.   Each heavy (armored) brigade is equipped with 58 Abrams tanks, 120 Bradley fighting vehicles, 120 M113-based vehicles, and 16 M109 self-propelled howitzers.

b.   Additional M113-based vehicles would be needed to equip division headquarters, fire brigades, and manueuver enhancement brigades. Additional M109 self-propelled howitzers would be needed to equip fire brigades.

c.   Sets of equipment sufficient for five brigade combat teams (BCTs) are prepositioned in various locations around the world to allow quick deployment of units. (BCTs, which the Army puts together for specific operations, are currently being replaced by modular heavy units. In 2003, they included between 3,000 and 5,000 soldiers and roughly 300 armored vehicles.)

d.   Represents vehicles needed at various locations for training soldiers in their use and maintenance and for replacing vehicles that are removed from units for repairs or upgrades or that are lost in accidents or in combat.

heavy brigade.[4] But unlike the premodular combat brigades, modular heavy brigades will have support units permanently assigned to them—which the Army argues will make modular brigades better able to operate independently. Moreover, under the modular structure, brigade combat teams will not have to be put together on an ad hoc basis when they are required for operations be-

cause team members will be permanently organized into a modular brigade.

Equipping Modular Units

The Army will need fewer armored vehicles to equip and support units under its modular structure than it required for premodular units in 2003. Because modular combat brigades are designed to be self-contained, standardized units, they will comprise more support forces and fewer combat forces—and thus more trucks and fewer armored

---

4.   A premodular combat battalion (such as an infantry or tank battalion) includes 600 to 800 soldiers.

vehicles—compared with a premodular mechanized infantry or armored brigade combat team (see Table 2-2 on page 19). That factor, plus the smaller number of heavy combat brigades in the Army in 2011, when the reorganization is complete, will yield a smaller requirement for armored vehicles in 2011 than in 2003 (see Table 2-3). That reduction could allow the Army to both retire some of its oldest armored vehicles, as it converts units to the modular design, and modernize heavy units that remain in the National Guard.

The Future Combat Systems Program

Although the Army's modularity initiative is designed to make its combat forces more flexible and responsive, the initiative will not enable them to deploy more quickly to remote trouble spots. The equipment proposed for a heavy modular brigade will weigh as much as the equipment associated with a typically equipped premodular armored or mechanized infantry brigade combat team. Therefore, transporting a modular heavy brigade will require the same amount and types of equipment as are needed to move a typical premodular heavy brigade combat team.

To address the obstacles to rapid deployment, the Army initiated the FCS program, which it regards as the cornerstone of its efforts to transform itself into the kind of force that the military needs in today's national security environment. The program, as the Army envisions it, would develop the next generation of combat vehicles to be as lethal and survivable as current weapons but to weigh much less and require far less fuel and other logistics support. The program would develop eight new manned armored vehicles as well as four classes of unmanned aerial vehicles, three types of unmanned ground vehicles, unattended ground sensors, a missile launcher, and a new munitions system, all of which would be linked by an advanced communications network into an integrated combat system of systems.

Manned FCS Vehicles

The eight types of manned FCS vehicles that the Army plans to develop are intended to replace the armored vehicles that currently equip its heavy combat units. (The design of those existing vehicles, as described in Chapter 1, dates from before 1980; moreover, especially in the case of the Abrams tank, the vehicles are very heavy and difficult to transport.) The missions and configurations of the eight new FCS vehicles would differ, but they would share a common chassis, engine, and other components and be much lighter and more fuel efficient than the armored vehicles in the Army's current fleet. The service argues that the common design will reduce the logistics burden—in terms of spare and replacement parts and required tools—associated with maintaining the eight different vehicles and that the FCS vehicles' greater fuel efficiency (relative to existing armored vehicles) should lessen the amount of refueling required on the battlefield.

The initial goal of the FCS program was to develop vehicles that could be transported by the Air Force's large fleet of C-130 aircraft, which would require that a vehicle weigh less than 20 tons. Although that may still be the program's ultimate goal, recent Army documents suggest that the weight limit for the initial design of the manned FCS ground vehicles has been relaxed and set at 24 tons.[5] Whether the ultimate weight of the vehicle will be 24 tons is an open question, but to meet even that goal, FCS vehicles would not be able to rely on heavy armor for protection. (The Army's existing armored vehicles, which are equipped with heavy armor, weigh far more than 24 tons: the latest models of the Abrams tank weigh 70 tons or more, and those of the Bradley fighting vehicle and M109 self-propelled howitzer weigh more than 30 tons.) Instead, to help them survive, FCS vehicles as envisioned by the Army would rely on knowledge of the enemy's whereabouts to avoid attacks and on active systems of protection that could detect and neutralize incoming projectiles.

The manned vehicles to be developed under the FCS program include seven variants that will replace all types of armored vehicles now in the Army's heavy units and one variant that has no current counterpart fielded in the Army's brigades (see Figure 2-1 and Table 2-4). The following descriptions of the various FCS vehicles are based on the Army's designs and requirements for the vehicles in early 2006.

---

5. See Office of the Secretary of Defense, *Future Combat Systems: Selected Acquisition Report* (September 30, 2005).

Figure 2-1.

Manned FCS Vehicles

Mounted Combat System	Infantry Carrier
NLOS Mortar	NLOS Cannon
Reconnaissance and Surveillance	Command and Control
Medical	Recovery and Maintenance

Source: Congressional Budget Office based on a presentation by Brigadier General Charles Cartwright and Dennis Muilenburg to the Science and Technology Panel of the Association of the United States Army, "One Team—Equipping Our Joint Warfighters with the World's Best Capability" (Williamsburg, Va., February 11, 2005).

Note: FCS = Future Combat Systems; NLOS = non-line-of-sight.

■ The mounted combat system (MCS) would replace the Abrams tank. Equipped with a new 120-millimeter gun capable of destroying targets at a distance of up to 8 kilometers, the MCS would weigh one-third as much as the latest model of the Abrams tank. Despite having one-fifth as much fuel-storage capacity as the Abrams, the MCS's cruising range, based on current designs, would be about two-thirds that of the tank (300 km as opposed to 440 km), and its maximum speed on roads (80 km per hour) would be about 20 percent greater.

■ The infantry carrier vehicle (ICV) is being designed to carry up to nine soldiers and two crew members and would replace some Bradley fighting vehicles and M113 armored personnel carriers in the current fleet. Compared with the Bradley, the ICV would be about

25 percent lighter, could cruise 70 percent as far on a tank of fuel that would be 40 percent smaller, and be capable of speeds almost 30 percent greater on roads. The ICV's cannon, at 30 mm, would be slightly larger and more powerful than the Bradley's 25 mm gun. Compared with the M113-based personnel carriers, the ICV would be roughly twice as heavy and have less than two-thirds of the cruising range but be able to travel at a higher speed. Since it would be equipped with a 30-mm cannon, however, the ICV would have greater firepower than the current M113-based vehicle, which is armed only with a machine gun.

■ As currently designed, the non-line-of-sight mortar (NLOS-M) would fire precision-guided mortar rounds and be able to operate 24 hours a day in all types of weather. Compared with the current M113-based mortar carrier that it would replace, the NLOS-M would be equipped with an improved machine gun and could travel 20 percent faster on roads. However, its cruising range would be roughly 60 percent less.

■ The non-line-of-sight cannon (NLOS-C) is designed to provide long-range fire to support combat battalions. It would replace the M109 self-propelled howitzers in combat brigades and, on the basis of current designs, would be capable of 50 percent faster rates of fire. The NLOS-C could travel 25 percent faster on roads, but its cruising range would be roughly the same as that of the M109 howitzer.

■ According to its current design, the reconnaissance and surveillance vehicle will feature a suite of advanced sensors to locate and identify enemy targets in all weather conditions, day or night. Like the ICV, it would be capable of slightly higher speeds than the Bradley fighting vehicle, but its range and fuel storage capacity would be about the same.

■ The command-and-control vehicle would provide commanders with the information and communications capability needed to command and control their subordinate forces while on the move. Compared with the M113-based command-and-control vehicle it would replace, the FCS vehicle would be able to travel at higher speeds and would carry an improved 25-mm machine gun.

Table 2-4.

FCS Replacements for Armored Vehicles in the Army's Modular Heavy Combat Brigades

Vehicle Mission	Vehicles in the Current Fleet		Manned FCS Vehicles	
	Name	Number	Name	Number
Combat	Abrams tank	58	Mounted combat system	60
Infantry Carrier	Bradley fighting vehicle	80	Infantry carrier vehicle	102
	M113-based vehicle	53	n.a.	n.a.
Mortar Carrier	M113-based vehicle	14	Non-line-of-sight mortar	24
Artillery	M109 self-propelled howitzer	16	Non-line-of-sight cannon	18
Scouting	Bradley fighting vehicle	40	Reconnaissance and surveillance vehicle	30
Command and Control	M113-based vehicle	44	Command-and-control vehicle	49
Medical	n.a.	n.a.	Medical vehicle	29
Recovery	M88 recovery vehicle	27	Recovery and maintenance vehicle	10
Total		**332**		**322**

Source: Congressional Budget Office based on Office of the Secretary of Defense, *Future Combat Systems: Selected Acquisition Report* (December 31, 2005); and data from the Department of the Army.

Note: FCS = Future Combat Systems; n.a. = not applicable.

■ The FCS medical vehicle (MedV), which is designed to provide advanced life support to critically injured soldiers while they are being evacuated from the battlefield, has no existing counterpart that has been fielded in large numbers with combat brigades. By comparison with the M113-based battlefield ambulance that is currently in the Army's inventory, the FCS MedV would provide greater capability to treat the wounded as they are being evacuated.

■ The FCS recovery and maintenance vehicle is being designed to transport repair crews around the battlefield and to recover disabled vehicles. Weighing 60 percent less than the M88 recovery vehicle it would replace in the Army's combat units, the FCS vehicle would have a cruising range roughly equal to that of the latest model of the M88 but a fuel tank one-quarter the size of that vehicle's.

Unmanned Aerial and Ground Vehicles

The FCS program would develop four classes of unmanned aerial vehicles (UAVs) to carry out surveillance, identify targets, and relay communications to the units that the UAVs support. According to the Army's current designs, the four classes, depending on the tasks they are

slated to perform, would vary by range and the length of time they could remain in the air (see Figure 2-2).

■ Class I UAVs would provide information to the individual soldier. The Army's current descriptions specify that it weigh less than 15 pounds, be able to take off and land vertically, have a range of 8 km, and be able to stay aloft for almost an hour.

■ Like Class I UAVs, Class II vehicles would also be capable of taking off and landing vertically but would have twice the range and endurance of the smaller UAVs. Class II UAVs, which would support commanders of infantry or MCS vehicle companies, are expected to weigh between 100 pounds and 150 pounds.

■ Class III UAVs are scheduled to replace the Shadow UAV that some Army units currently use and would provide information to battalion commanders. Current designs call for an aircraft that weighs 300 pounds to 500 pounds, has a range of 40 km, and is capable of staying aloft for six hours. Compared with the Shadow UAV, Class III UAVs could remain airborne longer and carry heavier payloads with more and better sensors, enabling them to find and identify more targets at greater distances.

Figure 2-2.

Unmanned FCS Aerial Vehicles

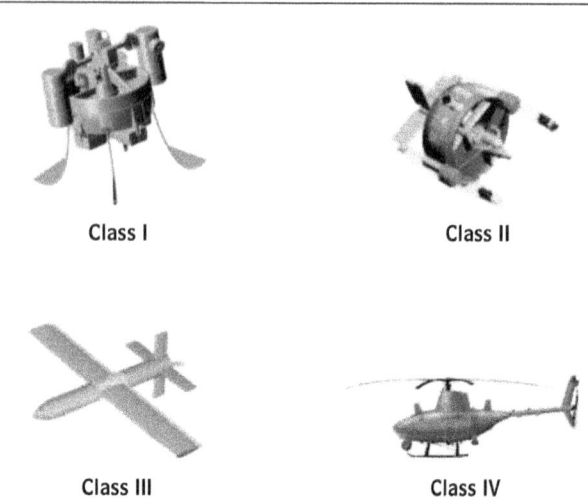

Class I   Class II

Class III   Class IV

Source: Congressional Budget Office based on a presentation by Brigadier General Charles Cartwright and Dennis Muilenburg to the Science and Technology Panel of the Association of the United States Army, "One Team—Equipping Our Joint Warfighters with the World's Best Capability" (Williamsburg, Va., February 11, 2005).

Note: FCS = Future Combat Systems.

■ Class IV UAVs, which are designed to support brigade commanders, would be produced in two versions. One would be capable of operating in tandem with Army helicopters; the other would be able to relay communications for as long as 24 hours and provide reconnaissance, early warning, and surveillance from a distance of as much as 75 km. Class IV UAVs could weigh more than 3,000 pounds and be as long as 23 feet.

Three types of unmanned ground vehicles, or robots, would also be developed under the FCS program (see Figure 2-3). In general, those vehicles are designed to lighten the loads of individual soldiers by performing continuous surveillance, carrying supplies, or entering areas of high risk.

■ The Army is developing two types of large armed robotic vehicles (ARVs), the initial versions of which are expected to weigh slightly more than 13 tons. Plans are for the assault variant (ARV-A) to provide remote reconnaissance and armed cover for soldiers and to deploy sensors and weapons in bunkers, buildings, and caves. According to the Army's current designs, the re-

connaissance, surveillance, and target acquisition variant of the ARV would carry additional sensors and communications equipment and provide remote reconnaissance of urban terrain and other dangerous locales.

■ Current designs call for the multifunctional utility, logistics, and equipment (MULE) vehicle—a 2.5-ton robot—to be built in three variants: the transport version, which would carry from 1,900 pounds to 2,400 pounds of soldiers' equipment; the countermine MULE, which would detect, mark, and defuse mines; and the ARV-assault-light, which would be a smaller, lighter version of the ARV-A.

■ The small unmanned ground vehicle (SUGV) is a robot designed to weigh less than 30 pounds and be carried by a soldier. The SUGV would carry as much as six pounds of equipment (typically, electronic sensors) for use in investigating caves, tunnels, buildings, or other potentially dangerous places. Early versions of this system are currently being used by soldiers in Iraq.

Unattended Sensors, the Launcher, Intelligent Munitions, and the Network

The remaining hardware systems in the FCS program are the unattended ground sensors, a missile launcher, and the intelligent munitions system (see Figure 2-4).

■ The unattended ground sensors—small modules equipped with relatively low-cost, expendable, multimodal sensors—are designed to detect intruders, chemicals, and biological agents and conduct surveillance in remote locations.

■ The non-line-of-sight launch system—a launch container equipped with 15 advanced missiles—is designed to be easily deployed and to be operated remotely or set for automated operations.

■ Plans for the intelligent munitions system (IMS) show it to be a system of sophisticated land mines equipped with sensors and communications links that would enable it to transmit information about personnel or vehicles whose presence it had detected. The mines could be turned on or off remotely and, to ensure that individual IMS units did not become residual hazards, would be designed to self-destruct on command or after a preset interval.

Figure 2-3.

Unmanned FCS Ground Vehicles

ARV-Assault   ARV-RSTA

MULE Transport Version   MULE Countermine Version

ARV-Assault (Light)   Small Unmanned Ground Vehicle

Source: Congressional Budget Office based on a presentation by Brigadier General Charles Cartwright and Dennis Muilenburg to the Science and Technology Panel of the Association of the United States Army, "One Team—Equipping Our Joint Warfighters with the World's Best Capability" (Williamsburg, Va., February 11, 2005).

Note: FCS = Future Combat Systems; ARV = armed robotic vehicle; MULE = multifunctional utility, logistics, and equipment; RSTA = reconnaissance, surveillance, and target acquisition.

The final but perhaps most important component of the FCS program is the network that, according to the Army, would "[allow] the FCS . . . to operate as a cohesive system of systems where the whole of its capabilities is greater than the sum of the parts."[6] The network would encompass the common operating software by which all FCS components would communicate with each other and share data; the communications and computer systems that would provide secure, reliable access to information over extended distances and complex terrain; and

intelligence and surveillance sensors that would allow weapon systems in an FCS-equipped brigade to avoid enemy fire, maintain contact with each other, and destroy adversaries at long range.

Schedule for Fielding FCS Components

Despite the wide diversity that characterizes the 18 individual systems of the FCS program, the Army initially planned to develop and field all of them in concert—a goal that the service has had to scale back to some extent, although the current schedule is still quite tight. The ambitiousness and complexity of the program have caused several changes in plans since it was first conceived. As described by then Army Chief of Staff General Eric Shinseki early in 2000 and laid out in an FCS program briefing in November 2002, the program would have included a short (three-year) system development and demonstration (SDD) phase starting in the spring of 2003.[7] All 18 systems were to enter production by 2006 and start initial fielding in 2008;[8] an ambitious procurement program would then follow, with annual purchases of three brigades' worth of all 18 FCS components. At that rate, General Shinseki predicted, all of the Army's combat brigades could be equipped with FCS components by 2032.

As the program approached the beginning of the SDD phase and a major review by the Office of the Secretary of Defense, the difficulty of meeting the schedule laid out by General Shinseki became apparent. The Army extended the SDD phase by almost two years and delayed until the second quarter of 2008 the decision about whether or not to begin production.[9] It also pushed back to 2011 the initial fielding of the 18 FCS components—or initial operating capability (IOC)—and reduced the rate of procurement to two brigades' worth of components per year rather than the three brigades' worth initially projected. At that rate, equipping the first 15 bri-

---

6.   U.S. Army Unit of Action Program Manager, *Future Combat Systems (FCS); 18+1+1 Systems Overview*, version 18 (September 15, 2005), p. 4.

---

7.   The SDD phase, as defined in this analysis, would extend from Milestone B (the terminology used in the Defense Department's acquisition programs to mark the program's entrance into the SDD phase) to Milestone C for manned vehicles—at which point approval to enter production would be granted by the Office of the Secretary of Defense.

8.   Briefing by the Army's Future Combat Systems Team's Program Review Board (November 12, 2002).

9.   Government Accountability Office, *Issues Facing the Army's Future Combat Systems Program*, GAO-03-1010R (August 2003).

Figure 2-4.

Other Unmanned FCS Systems

Unattended Ground Sensors

NLOS Launch System

Intelligent Munitions System

Source: Congressional Budget Office based on a presentation by Brigadier General Charles Cartwright and Dennis Muilenburg to the Science and Technology Panel of the Association of the United States Army, "One Team—Equipping Our Joint Warfighters with the World's Best Capability" (Williamsburg, Va., February 11, 2005).

Note: FCS = Future Combat Systems; NLOS = non-line-of-sight.

gades with FCS components would be delayed from 2015 (the original schedule) to 2020.

The program emerged from the review necessary to enter the SDD phase, in the spring of 2003, with additional changes. The time to be devoted to system development and demonstration was again extended, and a decision about whether to start production was delayed until November 2008.[10] The Army, reflecting concerns about the affordability of developing, testing, and producing all 18 FCS components on the tight schedule in place at the

program's entrance into the SDD phase, planned initially to introduce 14 of the 18 systems in 2011, with the understanding that the remaining four—the recovery and maintenance vehicle, two classes of UAVs, and the armed robotic vehicles—would be introduced later. Otherwise, the procurement and fielding schedule remained the same.

A restructuring of the program in July 2004 resulted in yet another schedule.[11] The Army introduced a new concept for the program that extended the SDD phase by almost four years and took into account (to some extent) the different levels of technical readiness of the various systems by introducing them in four phases—the Army called them spirals, or spin-outs—as the systems were proven. The plan as described in July 2004 was to first introduce parts of the network and three other systems—the unattended ground sensors, the intelligent munitions system, and the non-line-of-sight launch system—into one experimental unit for testing in 2008. If those tests proved successful, the three FCS components and the rudimentary network would be introduced into additional units. Two years later, in a second spiral, the Army would introduce a preliminary version of the Class III UAV, a prototype of the non-line-of-sight cannon, and additional portions of the network, first into the experimental unit and subsequently into other units. In 2012, it would introduce unmanned ground vehicles and in 2014, the remaining three classes of UAVs and final versions of all eight manned vehicles. In that way, the least technologically challenging components of the program would be introduced earlier, and the systems that were more difficult to develop could be deferred until later.

That approach pushed the fielding of the first brigade equipped with all 18 FCS components to 2015. After that, the Army planned to equip its combat brigades with the full complement of systems at a maximum rate of two brigades per year, as outlined in the Selected Acquisition

---

10. Statement of Paul L. Francis, Director, Acquisition and Sourcing Management, Government Accountability Office, before the Subcommittee on Tactical Air and Land Forces, Committee on Armed Services, House of Representatives, published as Government Accountability Office, *Defense Acquisitions: The Army's Future Combat Systems' Features, Risks, and Alternatives,* GAO-04-635T (April 1, 2004).

11. Statement of Paul L. Francis, Director, Acquisition and Sourcing Management, Government Accountability Office, before the Subcommittee on AirLand of the Senate Committee on Armed Services, published as Government Accountability Office, *Defense Acquisitions: Future Combat Systems—Challenges and Prospects for Success,* GAO-05-442T (March 16, 2005); and Andrew Feickert, *The Army's Future Combat System (FCS): Background and Issues for Congress,* CRS Report for Congress RL32888 (Congressional Research Service, April 28, 2005; updated May 5, 2006).

Figure 2-5.

Disposition of the Army's Heavy Brigades Under the Administration's Plan

(Number of brigades)

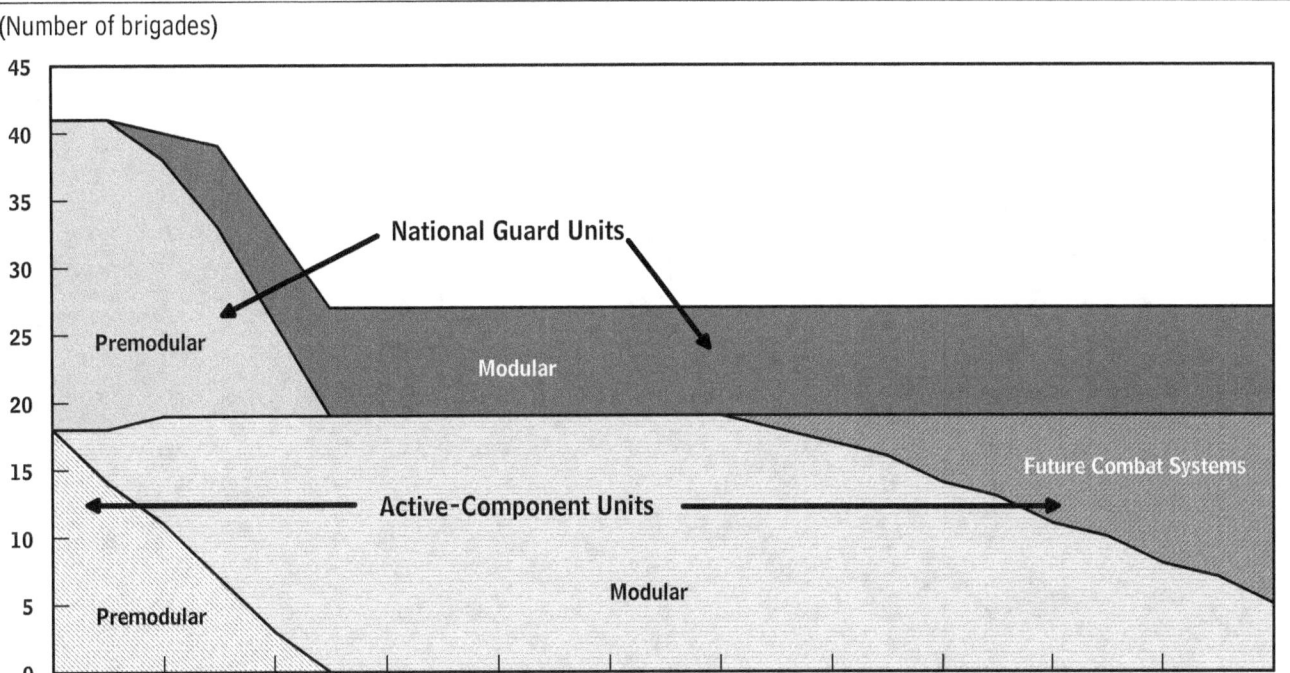

Source: Congressional Budget Office based on data from the Department of the Army and a private briefing by the Army titled "The Army Modular Force, 2004-2020" (July 2005).

Note: "Premodular" and "modular" refer to the Army's ongoing modularity initiative, which seeks to make the service more flexible by changing its structure from one based on 18 divisions, several of unique design, to one based on 70 combat brigades, each one of only three designs. "Heavy" units are those equipped with tracked armored vehicles.

Report (SAR) submitted to the Congress in December 2004.[12] Nine months later, the September 2005 SAR showed that the schedule had changed once again, and the Army's planned maximum rate for procuring FCS components had dropped to 1.5 brigades' worth per year. At that rate, the Army would have only six FCS-equipped

brigades in the field in 2020, and it would be 2026 before it fielded 15 such brigades (see Figure 2-5). Looking forward, if the Army continued to buy enough FCS components to equip 1.5 brigades per year, it would take until 2034 to equip all 27 of the Army's heavy brigades with the new systems—a very different outcome from that originally envisioned by General Shinseki in early 2000.[13]

12. The Department of Defense (DoD) provides Selected Acquisition Reports containing the department's projections of development schedules, purchase rates and quantities, and costs through the duration of a program. DoD is required by the Congress to provide SARs for major programs that meet certain guidelines.

13. An additional three years would be needed to equip five sets of prepositioned equipment with FCS components.

CHAPTER 3

Potential Effects of and Concerns About the Army's Modernization Plans

The Army's modularity initiative and the Future Combat Systems program could significantly transform the service, but a substantial investment is required to carry them out. This chapter examines how the two initiatives and the Army's continuing efforts to upgrade its armored vehicle fleet affect the service's costs, its ability to deploy units quickly, and the age and size of its armored combat vehicle fleet. The chapter also examines some of the questions and concerns that have been raised about the viability and feasibility of the FCS program.

How Modernization Plans Would Affect the Army's Budget

The FCS program is by far the most expensive modernization effort planned by the Army over the next 20 years. Based on the service's estimates in the Selected Acquisition Reports for the program issued in September and December 2005, the total cost from 2007 to 2025 to develop and procure the first 15 brigades' worth of FCS equipment would be $122 billion (in 2006 dollars). In contrast, the cost from 2007 through 2011 to convert all of the Army's combat brigades to a modular structure has been pegged at $54 billion. The Army has also budgeted several billion dollars for major upgrades to its armored vehicles during the next decade.

Cost of the FCS Program

The FCS program will require significant investment by the Army during the next 20 years. The research and development (R&D) portion of the program is scheduled to extend through 2016; according to the Army's current estimates, it will require annual funding exceeding $1 billion from 2007 through 2013 and topping $3 billion from 2007 through 2009. At those levels, R&D funding for the FCS program would represent more than one-third of the Army's total annual R&D budget for the five

years from 2007 through 2011. All told, the planned R&D investment in FCS components would require $21 billion during the 2007-2016 period.[1]

On the basis of information in recent SARs, the Congressional Budget Office estimates that the total cost for procuring the first 15 brigades' worth of FCS components will be about $100 billion and the average unit procurement cost will be $6.7 billion per brigade. Each FCS-equipped brigade would include roughly 300 manned vehicles, more than 230 unmanned ground vehicles, 112 unmanned aerial vehicle systems, and numerous additional unattended ground sensors, non-line-of-sight launch systems, and munitions (see Table 3-1 for details). Under the Army's current plan to purchase 1.5 brigades' worth of FCS components annually beginning in 2015, the FCS program would require $10 billion in that year and $8 billion to $10 billion annually thereafter—that is, for as long as the program continued purchases at that rate (see Figure 3-1).

Under that plan, the total funding required for the FCS program from 2007 through 2025 would be $140 billion, in CBO's estimation. That amount would include $21 billion for R&D and $119 billion to procure 18 brigades' worth of FCS equipment—enough to equip all but one of the heavy modular brigades planned for the Army's active component. Although the December 2005 SAR outlined funding for only 15 brigades' worth of equipment, the Army's intention at the inception of the FCS program in 2000 and as described in its 2002 modernization plan was to equip all of its combat brigades similarly. That goal would require purchasing 70 brigades' worth of FCS equipment, which at the rate of

---

1. Those estimates are based on the program described in the December 2005 SAR.

Table 3-1.

Planned New Components for an FCS-Equipped Brigade

	Quantity[a]
Manned Systems	
Mounted Combat System	60
Infantry Carrier Vehicle	102
Command-and-Control Vehicle	49
Reconnaissance and Surveillance Vehicle	30
Non-Line-of-Sight Mortar	24
Non-Line-of-Sight Cannon	18
Medical Vehicle	29
Recovery and Maintenance Vehicle	10
Unmanned Ground Vehicles	
Armed Robotic Vehicle-Assault	18
Armed Robotic Vehicle-Reconnaissance, Surveillance, and Target Acquisition	27
Armed Robotic Vehicle-Assault (Light)	18
Multifunctional Utility, Logistics, and Equipment Vehicle	90
Small Unmanned Ground Vehicle	81
Unmanned Aerial Vehicles (Launch and Control Units/Aircraft)	
Class I	54/108
Class II	36/36
Class III	12/48
Class IVa	2/8
Class IVb	8/16
Other	
Unattended Ground Sensors	136
Non-Line-of-Sight Launch System	60
Intelligent Munitions System	30 or 88[b]

Source: Congressional Budget Office based on Office of the Secretary of Defense, *Future Combat Systems: Selected Acquisition Report* (December 31, 2005).

Note: FCS = Future Combat Systems.

a. Does not include equipment for training or for replacing vehicles that are removed from units for repairs or upgrades or that are lost in accidents or in combat.

b. The Army has not yet determined whether each brigade will have 30 or 88 intelligent munitions systems.

1.5 brigades' worth per year could take until 2060. Even if the Army abandoned that goal and equipped only its heavy units (27 brigades) with FCS components, the program would extend its purchases until 2031 and have a

total acquisition cost (R&D plus procurement), starting in 2007, of almost $190 billion.

Cost of the Modularity Initiative

Because the Army's new modular units are designed to be equipped and staffed differently from the units they are scheduled to replace, the Army will have to purchase equipment and build facilities to carry out the reorganization of its forces. The total cost of the restructuring, based on the Army's estimates, would be $54 billion from 2007 through 2011 (see Table 3-2). The greatest share of that amount ($29 billion) would cover equipment for the new units, including either newly purchased or refurbished Abrams tanks, Bradley fighting vehicles, trucks and other support equipment, and large numbers of radios and other communications gear (see Table 3-3 on page 33).[2] Moreover, the Army might require as many as 30,000 additional personnel (at a cost of $16 billion), although the service has stated that they will be needed only through 2011. The remaining costs are associated with building new brigade facilities (for example, headquarters buildings and maintenance sheds) as new units are created or existing ones moved to new bases, and purchasing supplies for sustainment and training (for example, fuel, ammunition for training, and other expendable goods).

Cost of Planned Upgrades to Armored Combat Vehicles

The Administration's plan for upgrading vehicles in the Army's current fleet, as described in documents submitted with the President's budget for 2007, would require roughly $6 billion during the years 2007 to 2016.[3] Those funds would pay to modernize almost 90 Abrams tanks, bringing them to the A2 SEP (System Enhancement Pro-

---

2. The estimate of procurement costs for the Army's modularity initiative includes funds requested in the President's 2007 budget for upgrading the Army's tanks, Bradley fighting vehicles, and M113-based vehicles.

3. Plans through 2016 for upgrading Bradley fighting vehicles are described in the SAR for Bradley upgrades dated December 31, 2005; plans for the Abrams tanks and M113-based vehicles are available only through 2011. CBO's analysis covers only funds for major upgrades as requested in the procurement account of the Army's budget and does not include funds provided or requested in the operation and maintenance account. Those latter funds are generally used to support day-to-day maintenance and not efforts to modernize the armored combat vehicle fleet.

Figure 3-1.

Projected Total Annual Investment in the Future Combat Systems Program

(Billions of 2006 dollars)

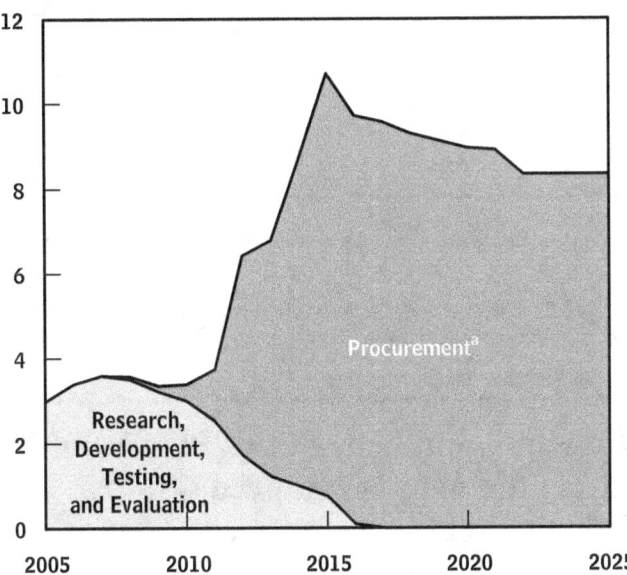

Source: Congressional Budget Office based on Office of the Secretary of Defense, *Future Combat Systems: Selected Acquisition Reports* (September 30 and December 31, 2005).

a.   Incorporates the assumption that the Army will continue to purchase 1.5 brigades' worth of FCS equipment indefinitely.

gram) configuration; roughly 1,600 Bradley fighting vehicles, upgrading them to the A2 ODS (Operation Desert Storm) or A3 model; and more than 840 M113-based vehicles, converting them to the A3 variant (see Table 3-4 on page 34). (The Army's budget does not include funds for any major upgrades to the M109 self-propelled howitzers.)

Many details of the Army's plans after 2011 are not yet available, but some briefings indicate that additional upgrades to its armored vehicles will incorporate technologies from the FCS program. Whether or not that occurs, the Army must continue to invest funds in its existing vehicles for many years if it is to keep them in good condition and up to date technologically. During the early part of this decade, the Army reportedly was reluctant to make such an investment because it was planning to replace all of its armored vehicles with FCS vehicles on an accelerated schedule. Now that the FCS schedule has been extended and the total number of brigades' worth of equipment has been reduced, that rationale for a lower level of investment no longer exists.

How Modernization Plans Would Affect the Army's Ability to Deploy Units Quickly

Although the Army's modularity initiative and the FCS program could help reduce the amount of heavy equipment in brigade-sized units, neither would significantly improve the speed at which those units could be deployed. The reason is that moving a modular heavy brigade, whether equipped with existing systems or FCS components, involves transporting more than 1,000 vehicles, including more than 300 tracked vehicles (primarily armored combat vehicles) and more than 500 trucks (see Table 3-5 on page 35). To be transported by air, an FCS-equipped brigade would require 340 to 370 C-17 sorties; if the destination was, for example, Djibouti, the process would take 18 to 20 days (see Table 3-6 on page 36).[4] A modular heavy brigade equipped with existing systems would require 420 sorties to deploy by air to Djibouti. Thus, replacing the tracked armored combat vehicles in the Army's current fleet with manned FCS vehicles would yield at most a 19 percent reduction in the airlift sorties (and time) needed to deploy a heavy unit overseas.

Brigade-sized units are rarely deployed alone, so it is useful to examine the time needed to deploy larger formations, such as divisions. *Premodular divisions* (described in Chapter 1) typically included three brigade combat teams and came in several types. In most cases, the equipment for a premodular heavy division totaled almost 100,000 tons, and although it required several sealift ships for transport, it could be moved by the Military Sealift Command's fleet in one sailing. Thus, a premodular heavy division that comprised three brigade combat teams could take roughly 110 days to deploy to Djibouti by air but could be sealifted there in less than 30 days (see Table 3-6 on page 36).

---

4.   That estimate is based on an average load of 50 tons to 55 tons per C-17, which would limit the number of manned FCS vehicles per sortie to two. The Army argues that it may be possible to load three manned FCS vehicles on a single C-17 aircraft. If that could be done, transporting an FCS brigade could require as many as 54 fewer C-17 sorties—and two to three fewer days—to transport it to Djibouti by air. Since the vehicles have not yet been built, however, it is not possible to determine how many would fit into a C-17. Furthermore, three FCS vehicles, each weighing 24 tons or more, would exceed a C-17's maximum allowable cabin load of 65 tons for a "leg" of 3,200 nautical miles.

Table 3-2.

Total Costs for the Army's Modularity Initiative

(Billions of 2006 dollars)

	2007	2008	2009	2010	2011	Total, 2007 to 2011
Equipment	5.3	5.7	6.1	6.2	5.4	28.6
Personnel	3.1	3.2	3.2	3.2	3.2	15.9
Facilities	0.5	0.5	1.4	1.4	1.4	5.1
Sustainment and Training[a]	0.7	1.1	1.0	0.9	0.8	4.5
Total	9.6	10.4	11.7	11.6	10.8	54.1

Source: Congressional Budget Office based on Government Accountability Office, *Force Structure: Actions Needed to Improve Estimates and Oversight of Costs for Transforming Army to a Modular Force,* GAO-05-926 (September 2005), p. 10.

Note: The Army's ongoing modularity initiative seeks to make the service more flexible by changing its structure from one based on 18 divisions, several of unique design, to one based on 70 combat brigades, each one of only three designs.

a.   Primarily, costs to purchase supplies, such as fuel, ammunition for training, and other expendable goods.

Although composed of smaller and generally lighter units, *modular divisions* comprise four combat brigades rather than three and may ultimately weigh more than their premodular counterparts. A modular heavy division with four modular heavy brigades could have almost 120,000 tons of equipment, or roughly 20 percent more than the amount assigned to a premodular heavy division—and that extra weight could significantly affect the time required to deploy the division by air. However, the additional equipment would not increase the time needed to deploy the division by sea because the additional 20,000 tons could be easily accommodated by the MSC's sealift fleet (see Table 3-6 on page 36).

An *FCS-equipped division*, according to the Army's current design, would be composed of four FCS-equipped brigades and weigh roughly 20 percent less than a modular heavy division.[5] Even so, transporting an FCS-equipped division by air to Djibouti would take at least 115 days. Moreover, it is unlikely that such a division could be transported by sea solely by the MSC's fleet of fast sealift ships. As a consequence, to deploy a division equipped with four FCS brigades to Djibouti by sea could take just as long as to deploy an entire modular heavy division to that location (see Table 3-6 on page 36).

---

5.   That estimate incorporates the assumption that units in the division other than combat brigades would be similarly equipped, regardless of the types of combat brigades that the division included.

How the Administration's Plan Would Affect the Army's Armored Combat Vehicle Fleet

Because the Army is not scheduled to begin to introduce manned FCS vehicles into its units until 2015 and then plans to continue to equip the units with the new systems at a relatively slow pace, the service is expected to retain many of the armored combat vehicles in its current fleet for at least 20 more years. The modularity initiative may allow the Army to reduce the size of the fleet and retire some of its oldest vehicles (see Chapter 2), but those remaining will have to be maintained in a serviceable condition for some time. In CBO's estimation, the effect of the upgrades that the Army plans to undertake between 2007 and 2016 will be small.

Effect of Planned Upgrades

The more than 2,500 upgrades that the Army plans to procure from 2007 through 2016 would improve the capabilities of its tanks, fighting vehicles, and personnel carriers and slightly lessen the increase in the average age of the armored vehicle fleet that would otherwise occur over that period. When combined with the additional upgrades funded in the supplemental appropriation enacted this past June, the planned upgrades would further the Army's efforts toward meeting its goal of having enough of the latest models of its Abrams tanks and Bradley fighting vehicles to equip all of its heavy brigades and prepositioned stocks. The planned upgrades, however, would result in an average age for the roughly 28,000 armored vehicles in the fleet (21 years in 2016) that was

Table 3-3.

Selected Items That the Army Plans to Buy to Implement Its Modularity Initiative

	Quantity
Trucks and Support Equipment	
High-Mobility Multipurpose Wheeled Vehicles (HMMWVs)	9,196
Medium Trucks	3,180
Heavy Trucks	1,148
Trailers for:	
HMMWVs	8,806
Medium trucks	5,455
Heavy trucks	3,169
Forward-Area Refueling Systems	4,630
Medical Systems	1,059
Generators	18,817
Assault Kitchens	646
Armored Vehicles[a]	
Abrams Tanks	512
Bradley Fighting Vehicles	1,260
M113-Based Vehicles	1,345
M88 Recovery Vehicles	170
Communications and Navigation Gear	
Global Positioning System Receivers	21,215
Single-Channel Ground and Airborne Radio System Radios	22,436
Joint Tactical Radio System Cluster 5 Radios	20,250
FBCB2 Systems	8,683
Other	
Night-Vision Goggles	98,053
Surface-Launched Advanced Medium-Range Air-to-Air Missile Air Defense Launchers	48
Unmanned Aerial Vehicles	21

Source: Congressional Budget Office based on Department of the Army, *The Army Modular Force and Future Combat Systems Strategy,* version 1.2 (undated).

Notes: The Army's ongoing modularity initiative seeks to make the service more flexible by changing its structure from one based on 18 divisions, several of unique design, to one based on 70 combat brigades, each one of only three designs.

FBCB2 = Future Battle Command Brigade and Below.

a. Purchases are upgrades to or recapitalization (complete overhaul) of existing equipment.

only slightly lower than would be the case without the upgrades (24 years).

Effect of Modularity

The Army's modularity initiative—combined with its elimination of unneeded vehicles—could significantly affect the armored combat vehicle fleet. CBO estimates that converting to the planned modular structure will reduce the Army's requirement for armored combat vehicles by more than a third—from upward of 23,000 in 2003 to fewer than 15,000 in 2011, when the reorganization is scheduled to be complete. If the Army chose to retire, or decommission, vehicles that were not needed to equip or support its heavy units, it could reduce the overall size of its armored combat vehicle fleet by about half, from approximately 28,000 vehicles in 2005 to roughly 14,500 vehicles in 2011 (see Figure 3-2 on page 37).

By eliminating more than 13,000 of its oldest vehicles between 2005 and 2011, the Army in that latter year could also reduce the average age of the fleet to 13 years instead of the 17 years that would result if all 28,000 armored vehicles were retained. If the Army chose to keep vehicles in its inventory that it did not need—and the Army has not retired large numbers of armored vehicles on such a compressed schedule in the past—it could mothball those older vehicles until they could be disposed of. The remaining smaller, or "active," fleet with its lower average age could then be used to equip and support the new modular units.[6]

Effect of the FCS Program

Manned FCS vehicles could ultimately replace most of the armored vehicles that now equip the Army's combat brigades. However, the Army would not begin to introduce the new vehicles until 2015 at the earliest, which in the context of the entire armored combat vehicle fleet would not significantly reduce the fleet's overall age. Even after significant numbers of FCS vehicles—roughly 500 per year starting in 2018—began to be fielded, the average age of the fleet would continue to increase (see Figure 3-3 on page 38).

---

6. Throughout this study, CBO uses the term "active fleet" to refer to those armored combat vehicles needed to equip and support the units in the modular Army.

Table 3-4.

Upgrades Included in the Administration's Plan for 2007 to 2016

System Upgrade	Quantity	Cost (Millions of 2006 dollars)
Abrams Tanks to the A2 SEP Model[a]	89	584
Bradley Fighting Vehicles		
To the A2 ODS model[a]	619	1,141
To the A3 model	998	4,081
M113-Based Vehicles to the A3 Model[a]	841	379
	2,547	6,184

Source: Congressional Budget Office based on Department of the Army, *Weapons and Tracked Combat Vehicles, Army: Committee Staff Backup Book, Fiscal Year 2007 Budget Estimates* (February 2006); and Office of the Secretary of Defense, *Bradley Upgrade: Selected Acquisition Report* (December 31, 2005).

Note: SEP = System Enhancement Program; ODS = Operation Desert Storm.

a. Upgrades are for the 2007-2011 period only.

How the introduction of FCS vehicles (as outlined in the Administration's plan) would affect the active fleet of 14,500 vehicles is more significant. Fielding 1.5 brigades' worth of FCS vehicles annually could keep the average age of the active fleet at or below 16 years during the 2011-2040 period (see Figure 3-4 on page 38).

According to the Army's latest schedule, FCS vehicles could conceivably replace all of the Abrams tanks, Bradley fighting vehicles, self-propelled howitzers, and M113-based vehicles in the Army's combat brigades and prepositioned stocks by 2037.[7] By then, the Army would have bought and fielded 32 brigades' worth of FCS vehicles—enough to equip all 27 heavy combat brigades in the Army's active component and the National Guard as well as an additional five brigades' worth of prepositioned stocks. As FCS vehicles were introduced and existing systems retired, the average age of the active armored combat vehicle fleet would begin to decrease, reaching a minimum of about 15 years when all of the systems currently equipping heavy combat brigades and prepositioned stocks had been retired.[8] At that point, the average age of

the active fleet would start to increase, as FCS vehicles that were initially introduced more than 20 years earlier remained in service.

Concerns Regarding the Army's FCS Program

Defense analysts, Members of Congress, and the Government Accountability Office have all expressed reservations about the FCS program. Among their concerns are the technological challenges facing developers of the FCS components, the affordability of the FCS program in the light of the Army's other funding needs, and the condition of the Army's current fleet of armored vehicles, which would be retained for several decades until they could be replaced by FCS vehicles.

Technological Readiness of FCS Components

Questions have arisen about whether the FCS program was ready to enter the system development and demonstration phase when it did, in the spring of 2003, and as a consequence whether the planned FCS components will be ready to go into production in 2012 as called for in the current schedule. The Department of Defense's (DoD's) acquisition policy requires that a technology needed for developing a weapon system meet certain criteria if it is to

---

7. That date is based on CBO's assumption that the Army ultimately hopes to equip all 70 combat brigades with FCS components and that it will continue to purchase those components at the rate of 1.5 brigades' worth per year even after the first 15 brigades' worth (Increment 1 of the procurement) have been bought. (The goal of equipping all of the Army's combat brigades was formulated by then Army Chief of Staff General Shinseki when the FCS program was initiated in 2000.)

8. Several hundred M113-based vehicles and M109 self-propelled howitzers would be retained to equip units other than combat brigades.

Table 3-5.

Comparing the Army's Premodular Heavy Brigade Combat Teams, Modular Heavy Combat Brigades, and Brigades Equipped with Future Combat Systems

	Premodular Heavy Brigade Combat Team	Modular Heavy Combat Brigade	FCS-Equipped Brigade
Personnel (Number)	3,800	3,800	3,300
Vehicles (Number)[a]			
Tracked	450	370	320
Trucks	840	880	550
Towed	390	410	180
Other[b]	10	20	180 [c]
Total Vehicles	**1,690**	**1,680**	**1,230**
Weight, All Equipment (Tons)	25,000	25,000	18,700
Coverage, All Equipment (Thousands of square feet)	323	320	260 to 290
Deployment of Equipment			
By air (Number of C-17 sorties)[d]	420	420	340 to 370
By sea (Number of ships)[e]			
Fast sealift	3	3	2
Large medium-speed roll-on/roll-off	2	2	1

Source: Congressional Budget Office based on data from the Department of the Army and Military Traffic Management Command Transportation Engineering Agency, *Deployment Planning Guide: Transportation Assets Required for Deployment,* MTMCTEA Pamphlet 700-5 (May 2001).

Note: "Premodular" and "modular" refer to the Army's ongoing modularity initiative, which seeks to make the service more flexible by changing its structure from one based on 18 divisions, several of unique design, to one based on 70 combat brigades, each one of only three designs. "Heavy" units are those equipped with tracked armored vehicles.

a.   Numbers are rounded to the nearest 10 vehicles.

b.   Includes helicopters and wheeled vehicles that cannot drive for long distances on roads.

c.   Includes 150 unmanned ground vehicles and 20 armed reconnaissance helicopters in addition to wheeled vehicles that cannot drive for long distances on roads.

d.   Based on an average load of 60 tons for heavy units and 50 tons to 55 tons for FCS-equipped combat brigades and rounded to the nearest 10 sorties.

e.   Either fast sealift ships or large medium-speed roll-on/roll-off ships will be needed but not both. Numbers of ships are rounded up to the nearest whole ship.

be considered "mature": it should have been demonstrated in a relevant environment—referred to as attaining technology readiness level (TRL) 6—or, preferably, have been demonstrated in an operational environment (TRL 7).[9] By the time the FCS program entered the SDD phase, the Army had identified 31 technologies that

it judged were critical to the development of the FCS components.[10] However, at that point, only one of those technologies had matured beyond TRL 6, and an additional seven critical technologies (23 percent) had attained TRL 6. According to GAO, "best practices of leading commercial firms and successful DoD programs have

9.   Technology readiness levels were pioneered by the National Aeronautics and Space Administration and subsequently adopted by DoD to measure whether technologies were sufficiently mature to be incorporated in a weapon system. See Appendix C for definitions of the TRLs.

10.   The Army defines a critical technology as one that is new or that is required in a new application to enable the FCS components to meet the operational requirements established for them. Appendix C lists the critical technologies applicable to the FCS program.

Table 3-6.

Time Needed to Deploy Equipment of Combat Units to East Africa

(Days)

	Airlift[a]	Sealift
Brigade-Sized Units		
Premodular Armored Brigade Combat Team with Existing Armored Vehicles	23	25
Modular Heavy Brigade with Existing Armored Vehicles	23	25
FCS-Equipped Brigade	18-20	25
Division-Sized Units[b]		
Three Premodular Armored Brigade Combat Teams with Existing Armored Vehicles	110	27
Four Modular Heavy Brigades with Existing Armored Vehicles	135	27
Four FCS-Equipped Brigades	115-130	27

Source: Congressional Budget Office based on data from the Department of the Army; Military Traffic Management Command Transportation Engineering Agency, *Deployment Planning Guide: Transportation Assets Required for Deployment,* MTMCTEA Pamphlet 700-5 (May 2001); and Department of the Air Force, *Air Mobility Planning Factors,* Pamphlet 10-1403 (December 18, 2003).

Notes: Units would be moved from the continental United States. The data do not reflect the time needed to move sustaining units or supplies.

"Premodular" and "modular" refer to the Army's ongoing modularity initiative, which seeks to make the service more flexible by changing its structure from one based on 18 divisions, several of unique design, to one based on 70 combat brigades, each one of only three designs.

FCS = Future Combat Systems.

a. The number of daily sorties constrained by the capacity of the airfield in East Africa, based on average airlift payloads per brigade of 60 tons for heavy units and 50 tons to 55 tons for FCS-equipped units.

b. Besides combat brigades, divisions include headquarters and other support units.

shown that critical technologies should be mature to at least a TRL 7 before the start of product development."[11] Nevertheless, the FCS program entered the SDD phase in May 2003.

Despite the fact that the Army has restructured the FCS program several times since May 2003 and lengthened the time allotted to the SDD phase, GAO has criticized the ambitious schedule that the service proposes for developing and fielding the 18 FCS components. GAO officials testified in March 2005 that the schedule for the program that the Army was proposing at that time would require developing multiple systems and a network in the same amount of time that DoD typically spends in developing a single advanced system.[12]

Pace of Development. Even though the FCS program has progressed technologically since May 2003, concerns about the level of maturity of its systems persist. If everything were to go according to the Army's plan, the FCS program would attain the level of technological readiness that it should have had before it entered the SDD phase—that is, all technologies judged to be at TRL 6 or higher—in 2009. But everything has not gone as planned, and the development of some critical technologies has been slower than anticipated. In October 2004, the Army assessed the critical technologies (which by then numbered 54) needed to develop the FCS components. It concluded that more than a year after entering the SDD phase, only one technology had attained TRL 7 or above.[13] And the fraction of all critical technologies attaining TRL 6 or higher remained roughly the same as it had been when the program entered the SDD phase a year earlier.

---

11. Government Accountability Office, *Defense Acquisitions: Improved Business Case Is Needed for Future Combat System's Successful Outcome,* GAO-06-367 (March 2006), p. 17.

12. Statement of Paul L. Francis, Director, Acquisition and Sourcing Management, Government Accountability Office, before the Subcommittee on AirLand of the Senate Committee on Armed Services, published as Government Accountability Office, *Defense Acquisitions: Future Combat Systems—Challenges and Prospects for Success,* GAO-05-442T (March 16, 2005).

13. Office of the Deputy Assistant Secretary of the Army for Research and Technology, *Future Combat Systems (FCS) Increment 1 Technology Readiness Assessment (TRA) Update* (October 2004).

Figure 3-2.

Average Age and Composition of the Active Armored Combat Vehicle Fleet

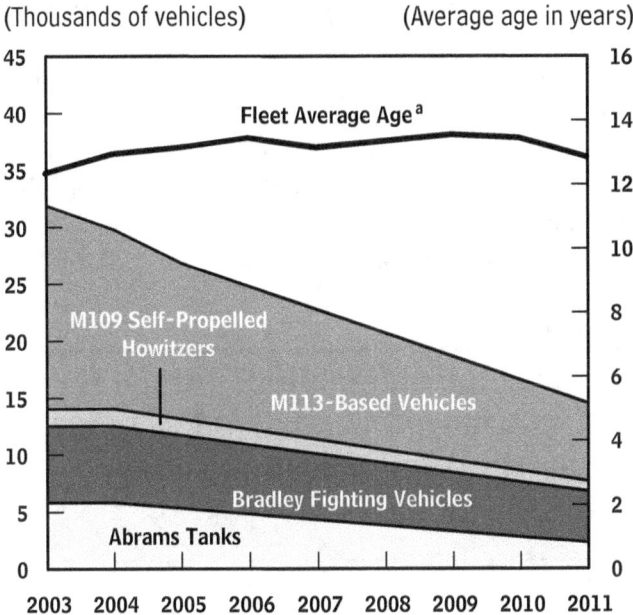

(Thousands of vehicles)   (Average age in years)

Source: Congressional Budget Office based on data from the Department of the Army.

Note: The "active fleet" comprises all models of the vehicles that CBO estimates will be needed to equip and support modular units in both the Army's active component and the Army National Guard. (Modular units are those resulting from the Army's ongoing modularity initiative, which seeks to make the service more flexible by changing its structure from one based on 18 divisions, several of unique design, to one based on 70 combat brigades, each one of only three designs.)

a.   Reflects upgrades to existing systems based on documents submitted with the President's 2007 budget.

In addition to assessing the program's current status in such reports, the Army has also estimated when technologies might attain the required readiness levels. But the service's past predictions have not been accurate. A relatively recent assessment (dated April 2005) of the technologies' maturity showed that progress in achieving technical readiness, although noticeable, had been less than the October 2004 assessment predicted.[14] When many of the technologies that the assessment projected

would achieve TRL 6 by 2006 were subsequently evaluated in April 2005, the Army then predicted that they would achieve that level as many as three years later. Moreover, that prediction was made despite the fact that the number of technologies considered critical to developing the FCS components had been reduced. As the April 2005 assessment reports, five of the more challenging critical technologies—which were far from maturity at the time of the October 2004 assessment—have now been dropped from the list (see Appendix C for more details).[15]

The history of technologies associated with the communications equipment that FCS components will incorporate—specifically, software-programmable radios—illustrates the challenges that the Army faces in carrying out its modernization plans. The technologies for software-programmable radios were judged to have attained TRL 6 in May 2003. The Army's subsequent assessment of those technologies in October 2004 put their level of maturity at TRL 5 but predicted that they would reach TRL 6 in 2006.[16] The Army's April 2005 assessment, however, indicated that those technologies might not reach TRL 6 before 2007. Such setbacks reinforce the conclusion by GAO and the Army's independent review team that the schedule established for developing all 18 FCS components in the time DoD typically takes to develop a single system is a risky one.

Varying Technological Challenges Posed by Different FCS Components. The development of individual FCS components does not necessarily require that all 49 critical technologies be mature. (For example, the development of unmanned aerial vehicles does not rely on the kind of technologies—such as lightweight hulls and armor—that would be needed for the development of manned and unmanned ground vehicles.) It is fair to assume, however, that the greater the number of mature technologies required to develop a system, the greater the risk that the system will not be ready on schedule.

---

14. Office of the Deputy Assistant Secretary of the Army for Research and Technology, *Technology Readiness Assessment Update* (April 2005), cited in Government Accountability Office, *Defense Acquisitions: Improved Business Case Is Needed*, p. 16.

15. The five technologies that the Army no longer considers necessary for the initial fielding of the FCS components are the ability to generate water from vehicle exhaust, the ability to rapidly assess damage inflicted on enemy targets as a result of U.S. attacks, and three technologies that would have helped soldiers reliably identify friends and foes in combat.

16. Those technologies are necessary for the development and fielding of Clusters 1 and 5 of the Joint Tactical Radio System and the Warfighter Information Network-Tactical.

Figure 3-3.

Average Age and Composition of the Armored Combat Vehicle Fleet Under the Administration's Plan

(Thousands of vehicles)   (Average age in years)

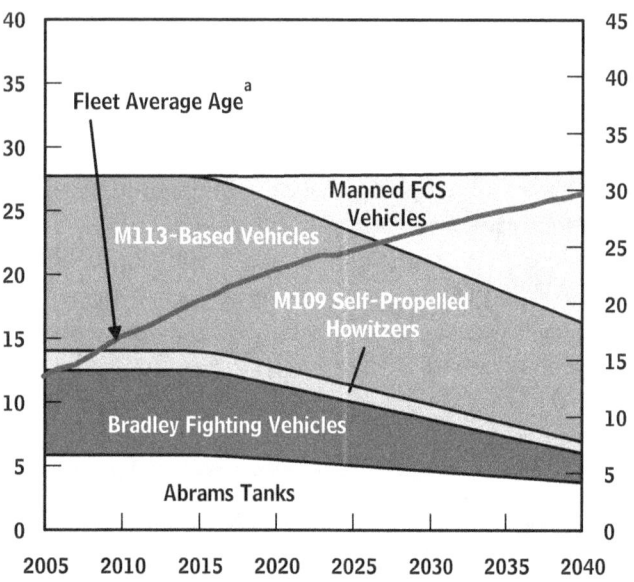

Source: Congressional Budget Office based on data from the
          Department of the Army.

Notes: Vehicle inventories represent totals of all models owned by
        the Army.

        FCS = Future Combat Systems.

a. Reflects upgrades to existing systems based on documents sub-
    mitted with the President's 2007 budget.

The number of technologies needed to develop each of the various FCS components and the network can be used to gauge the relative technical challenge that each system poses. Based on that measure, the manned ground vehicles are the most technologically complex, requiring the maturity of 17 critical technologies. By comparison, the systems that the Army is planning to field first (the non-line-of-sight launch system, the unattended ground sensors, and the intelligent munitions system) are the least problematic because they depend on the maturity of only two critical technologies (see Figure 3-5 and Appendix C, which maps critical technologies to types of systems). In between, in order of increasing technical so-phistication, are the UAVs (for which a very small, light-weight engine and a communications relay device are needed) and the unmanned ground vehicles (which re-quire development of autonomous navigation systems,

lightweight hulls, and mine-detection sensors and tech-nologies for destroying or neutralizing mines). The net-work presents the most challenges: to make it fully func-tional requires that 27 critical technologies be mature, and by the end of 2005, only 11 had achieved TRL 6.

The varying levels of technical maturity were part of the reason that the Army decided in the summer of 2004 to introduce the 18 systems in four phases, or spirals, to have additional time to develop the more technologically difficult systems. Similarly, increasingly demanding versions of the network are scheduled to be fielded in

Figure 3-4.

Average Age and Composition of the Active Armored Combat Vehicle Fleet Under the Administration's Plan

(Thousands of vehicles)   (Average age in years)

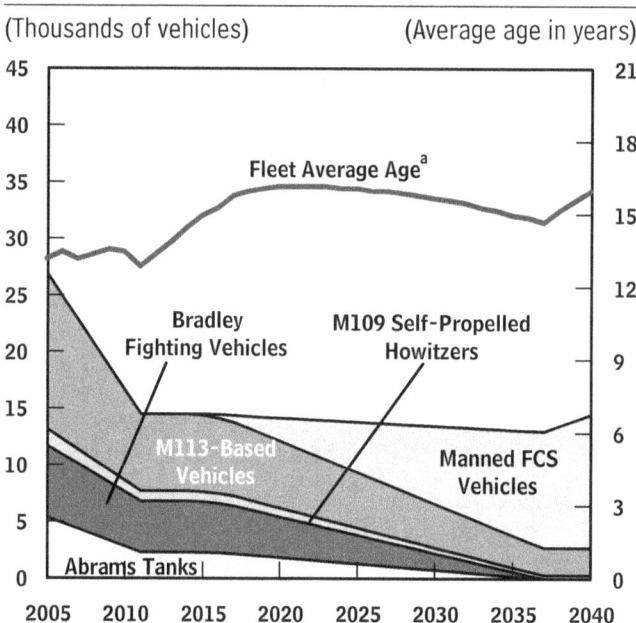

Source: Congressional Budget Office based on data from the
          Department of the Army.

Note: The "active fleet" comprises all models of the vehicles that
        CBO estimates are needed to equip and support modular
        units in both the Army's active component and the Army
        National Guard. (Modular units are those resulting from the
        Army's ongoing modularity initiative, which seeks to make
        the service more flexible by changing its structure from one
        based on 18 divisions, several of unique design, to one
        based on 70 combat brigades, each one of only three
        designs.)

a. Reflects upgrades to existing systems based on documents sub-
    mitted with the President's 2007 budget.

Figure 3-5.

Status of Critical Technologies for FCS Components at the End of 2005

(Number of technologies)

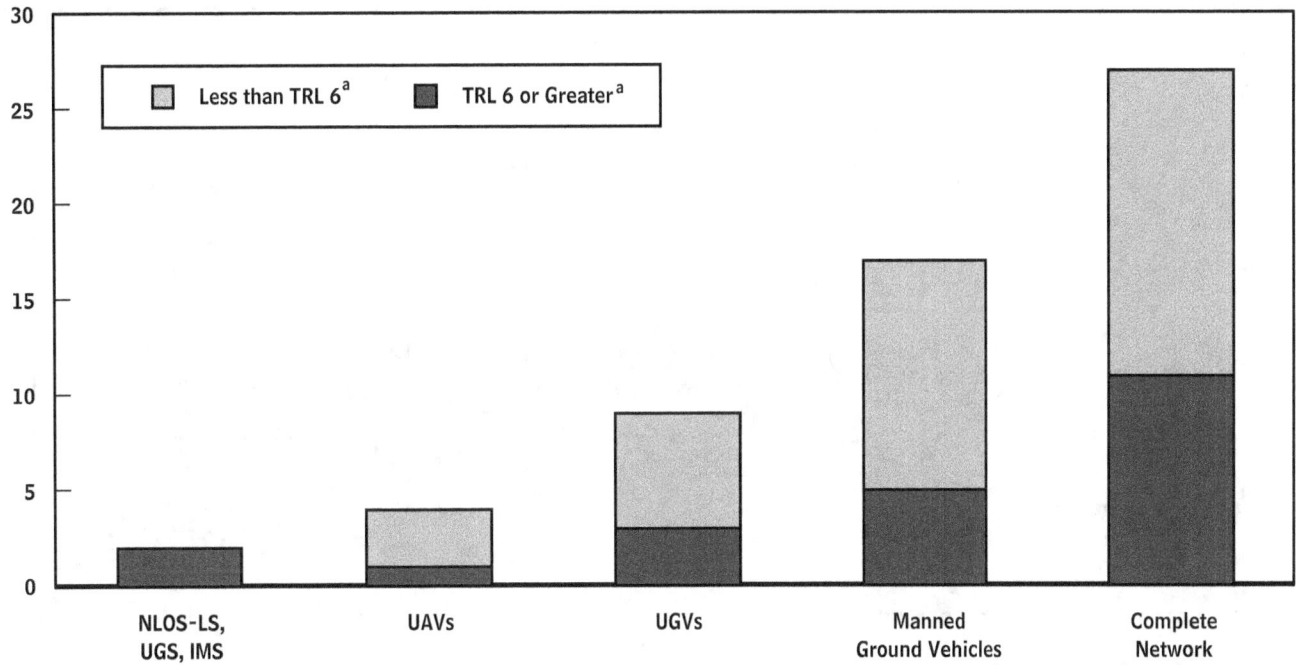

Source: Congressional Budget Office based on data from the Department of the Army and Office of the Deputy Assistant Secretary of the
           Army for Research and Technology, *Future Combat Systems (FCS) Increment 1 Technology Readiness Assessment (TRA) Update*
           (October 2004).

Note: A critical technology, according to the Army, is one that is new or that is required in a new application to enable the FCS components
           to meet the Army's operational requirements.

           FCS = Future Combat Systems; NLOS-LS = non-line-of-sight launch system; UGS = unattended ground sensors; IMS = intelligent
           munitions system; UAV = unmanned aerial vehicle; UGV = unmanned ground vehicle.

a.   For a technology to be considered mature enough to use in developing a weapon system, the Department of Defense's (DoD's) acquisition
      policy recommends that it be successfully demonstrated in a relevant environment, a criterion referred to as achieving TRL (technology
      readiness level) 6. (TRL measures were pioneered by the National Aeronautics and Space Administration and subsequently adopted by
      DoD.)

increments along with increasingly sophisticated FCS
components.

Development of Software. Another technological hurdle
that the Army must overcome is development of the software that will allow all of the FCS components to communicate with each other, share data, and operate with
existing systems. At least 34 million lines of software code
must be generated, or about twice the amount needed for
the Joint Strike Fighter, DoD's largest software undertak-
ing to date. According to GAO, the software required for
the overall operating environment may not reach the level
of technical maturity necessary in time to meet the scheduled milestones in the FCS program—which makes the

successful development of that common environment
uncertain.[17] Furthermore, because broad requirements
for the FCS components were still evolving in mid-2005,
the more-detailed specifications required to write software had not yet been established. Consequently, GAO
also reported in June 2005 that it was unclear whether
the software would be sufficiently developed to support
the fielding of the first spiral of FCS components in
2008.

_____

17. Government Accountability Office, *Defense Acquisitions: Resolving
    Development Risks in the Army's Networked Communications Capa-
    bilities Is Key to Fielding Future Force*, GAO-05-669 (June 2005).

Figure 3-6.

The Army's Major Procurement Programs and Budget Through 2025

(Billions of 2006 dollars)

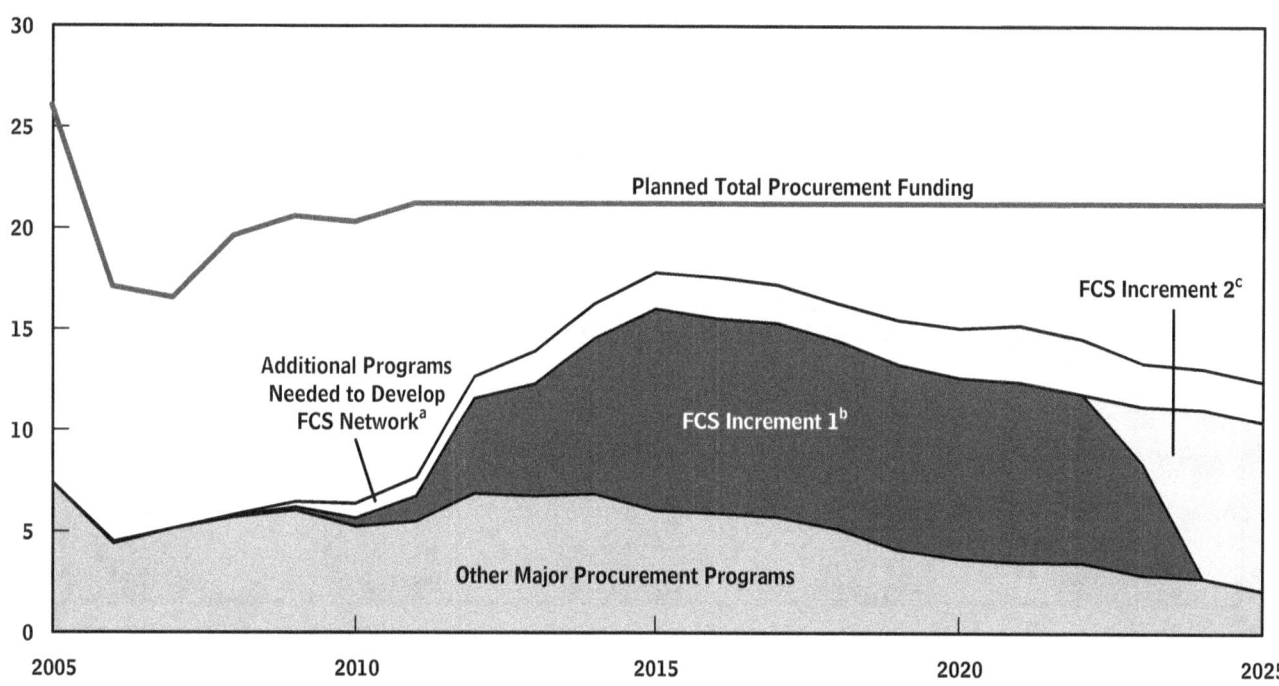

Source: Congressional Budget Office based on Office of the Secretary of Defense, *Selected Acquisition Reports,* various systems
                (September 30, 2005, and December 31, 2005).

Notes: Major procurement programs are those for which the Army is required to submit Selected Acquisition Reports to the Congress.

            FCS = Future Combat Systems.

a.   Includes the Joint Tactical Radio System Clusters 1 and 5 and the Warfighter Information Network-Tactical program.

b.   Under this phase of the FCS program, the Army would purchase a total of 15 brigades' worth of FCS equipment at a rate of 1.5 brigades'
        worth per year.

c.   During this phase, the Army would continue to purchase 1.5 brigades' worth of FCS components annually through 2025.

Affordability of the FCS Program

Funding for the FCS program will consume a significant portion of the Army's procurement budget well into the 2020s. According to the latest SARs, the FCS program will require $8 billion to $10 billion annually starting in 2015 (when the Army would start to buy 1.5 brigades' worth of equipment each year). During the preceding five years, the FCS program would consume increasingly larger amounts of the service's procurement funding (see Figure 3-6). In 2011, planned FCS costs would account for about 6 percent of the Army's $21 billion procurement budget, CBO estimates; by 2015, that share could rise to almost half and remain at or above 40 percent through 2025. (For purposes of comparison, in the mid-1980s, at the height of the Reagan defense buildup, the

Army dedicated at most 20 percent of its procurement funds to buy combat vehicles.)

Devoting such a large portion of its procurement funding to the FCS program would leave the Army little to invest in other weapon systems (such as upgrades to its tanks) or to purchase needed support equipment (such as small trucks, generators, and ammunition).[18] In 2008, the Army is slated to spend almost $14 billion of its total $20 billion in procurement funds on smaller programs that are not required to submit SARs to the Congress. In

---

18. CBO's analysis, like similar studies by the Army and GAO, incorporates the assumption that after 2011, the Army's procurement account will grow at the rate of annual inflation.

addition to the FCS program, the Army has allocated large amounts of its future procurement funds to other major programs (such as the Warfighter Information Network-Tactical, the Joint Tactical Radio System, and the Blackhawk helicopter). Given the budgetary demands of those programs and under the assumption (which the Army incorporates in its analyses) that the procurement account will grow at the rate of inflation after 2011, only $3 billion would be available in the account in 2015—compared with $14 billion in 2008—to pay for the many items that the Army needs, such as ammunition, generators, trailers, and many other goods.[19]

Past Cost Growth. The FCS program has experienced a significant increase in costs since it entered the SDD phase in the spring of 2003. At that time, Army estimates put the cost of a program to develop and purchase the FCS network and all of the components except the recovery and maintenance vehicle in quantities sufficient to equip 15 brigades (from 2005 through 2025) at $80 billion. One and a half years later, in the December 2004 SAR, the program's estimated costs over the same period had risen slightly, to $83 billion, on the basis of plans that reduced the scope of the effort to 14 systems and the network and delayed it by one year. Just nine months later, in September 2005, the Army announced that the cost from 2005 through 2025 of developing and procuring all 18 components and the network for the first 15 brigades had jumped to $128 billion, a 60 percent increase over the original estimate of $80 billion. At the same time, the Army reduced the maximum annual rate of procurement of FCS components from two brigades' worth of equipment to 1.5 brigades' worth.[20]

Risk of Additional Cost Growth. The costs of the FCS program could continue to grow, if those of past major defense programs are any guide. In analyses of historical trends in the costs of DoD's weapon programs, RAND and the Institute for Defense Analyses (IDA) demonstrated that R&D costs grew from 16 percent to about 70 percent and procurement costs rose by between 11 percent and roughly 70 percent, as measured from estimates prepared when the program entered the SDD phase. (The higher end of those ranges reflects cost growth experienced by ground vehicles; see Appendix D for further discussion of historical cost growth rates and RAND's and IDA's analyses.) If, as GAO and others

maintain, the FCS program entered the SDD phase prematurely—in part because the program at that time was still insufficiently well defined—historical precedent suggests that costs for the program could continue to grow at high rates. Because the FCS program is developing and procuring several different types of systems, CBO used a weighted average of the rates of cost growth that apply to different types of systems to determine an estimated rate of overall cost growth risk—roughly 60 percent. That rate reflects the fact that ground vehicles are the most costly component of the FCS program and in the past experienced rates of cost growth that exceeded 70 percent.

If costs for the FCS program grew as those for similar programs have in the past, the annual funding needed from 2015 through 2025 could rise from the current estimate of $8 billion to $10 billion to $13 billion to $16 billion. From 2015 to 2022, the Army intends to procure 1.5 brigades' worth of FCS components each year, a plan that could require $15 billion annually in the years from 2016 to 2018 if costs grew at historical rates. The total funds allotted to the Army's procurement account in 2011 are currently estimated at $21 billion (in 2006 dollars) and if the account grew only at the rate of inflation would remain at that level. Devoting $15 billion—or more than 70 percent—of that amount solely to purchases of FCS components in 2016 would leave just $6 billion in procurement funds for other programs, both large and small, that are currently slated to receive a total of $20 billion in 2011.

---

19. Based on Department of the Army, *The Army Modular Force and Future Combat Systems Strategy* (undated), p. 15.

20. An independent estimate of the cost of the FCS program submitted to the Congress in June 2006 by the Cost Analysis Improvement Group (CAIG) in the Office of the Secretary of Defense indicates that the costs of the program may be higher than the latest Army estimates suggest. The CAIG estimated that R&D costs could range from $34 billion to $47 billion and procurement costs might be $126 billion (all costs are in 2006 dollars). Because the CAIG's estimate includes some procurement costs that are not included in the Army's figures, the two estimates may not be totally comparable. But the additional items that the CAIG included and the Army did not (missiles and munitions for training and war reserves as well as funds for some modifications) are not likely to represent a significant portion of the CAIG's overall estimate of procurement costs. In any case, the CAIG indicated in its report that its June 2006 estimate represented an increase of more than 70 percent over its estimate of the costs of the FCS program made in the spring of 2003, prior to the program's entry into the SDD phase. See Office of the Secretary of Defense, Cost Analysis Improvement Group, "Report to Congress on Future Combat Systems: Independent Cost Estimate" (June 2006).

Potential Reductions in Procurement Rates for FCS Components. The Army has already amended the schedule for the FCS program to address concerns about affordability, reducing the maximum annual rate of purchases from three brigades' worth (as proposed in November 2002) to 1.5 brigades' worth (established in September 2005). Despite those reductions, the annual cost of the program would remain above $8 billion in 2014 and for several years thereafter. If costs continued to grow, the rate of annual purchases might need to be further reduced.

As an example of purchases under a less expensive program, the Army could buy a maximum of one brigade's worth of equipment per year. At that rate, components to equip the initial increment of 15 brigades would not be purchased until 2027 and would not be fully fielded until 2030. Of course, the annual funding for the FCS program would also be reduced from the levels outlined in the latest SARs ($8 billion to $10 billion) to $5 billion to $7 billion (see Figure 3-7). If, however, program costs grew at a rate typical of such development and procurement efforts, the annual funding requirements would still be substantial—on the order of $10 billion, or roughly the estimated costs, but without potential growth, outlined in the September 2005 SAR for buying 1.5 brigades' worth of components per year.

Concerns About Maintaining the Army's Current Fleet of Armored Vehicles
The total size of the FCS program—in terms of brigades' worth of equipment purchased—and the rate at which the program is executed will determine how many of the Army's existing fleet of armored vehicles will be retained and for how long. As mentioned earlier, the Army at the end of 2005 still maintained a sizable armored combat vehicle fleet (approximately 5,850 Abrams tanks, 6,650 Bradley fighting vehicles, 13,700 M113-based vehicles, and roughly 1,500 M109 self-propelled howitzers). FCS components would begin to replace some of those vehicles in 2015, but for armored vehicles in the combat brigades and in the prepositioned equipment sets, the process would not be complete until 2037 at the earliest, and until then, existing vehicles would have to be maintained. Some M113-based vehicles and M109 howitzers that equip units other than combat brigades might be retained indefinitely.

The Army's budgetary plans, however, do not include sufficient funds to maintain all of the vehicles it currently has in its inventory. In fact, on the basis of the upgrades noted in plans submitted with the President's 2007 budget and the schedule for introducing manned FCS vehicles into units, CBO estimates that the average age of the Army's total fleet of armored combat vehicles could reach 23 years by 2020 and 30 years by 2040 (see Figure 3-3 on page 38).

A more useful measure of the status of the Army's armored combat vehicle fleet might be the average age of the active vehicle fleet. As discussed earlier, the Army's modularity initiative will reduce the total number of vehicles that the service needs; CBO estimates that if the service used only the latest versions of the armored vehicles in its current fleet, the average age of the active fleet (approximately 14,500 vehicles rather than the total fleet of 28,000 vehicles) would be 16 years in 2020 and would remain at or below that level through 2040 (see Figure 3-4 on page 38). Even though the average age of the active fleet would be much lower than the average age of the entire inventory, it would still almost always exceed 15 years after 2015, the age that the Army considers the top of the desirable range.

Cost of Additional Upgrades. The average age of the armored combat vehicle fleet could be reduced if the Army invested in upgrades for its existing vehicles. To keep the average age of the fleets of existing vehicles relatively constant after 2011, the Army must, in CBO's estimation, upgrade and overhaul roughly 800 Abrams tanks, 2,500 Bradley fighting vehicles, 3,000 M113-based vehicles, and 550 M109 howitzers between 2007 and 2025, investing $21 billion over that period.[21] If it did so, the service could reduce the average age of its active fleet of combat vehicles from more than 15 years in 2016 without those additional upgrades to one that would be consistently below 13 years through 2040 (see Figure 3-8).

Effect of a Diminished FCS Program. If the Army's concerns about affordability persuaded it to stretch out the FCS program or truncate it at 15 brigades' worth of

---

21. Such investments—which include those requested in the President's budget for 2007—would either upgrade a less capable model to the most capable model or, for a vehicle that was already the latest model, totally overhaul it so that its age would be reset to zero. For details of CBO's estimates of the costs to upgrade existing armored combat vehicles, see Appendix D.

Figure 3-7.

Estimated Total Annual Costs for the Future Combat Systems Program Including Potential Cost Growth

(Billions of dollars)

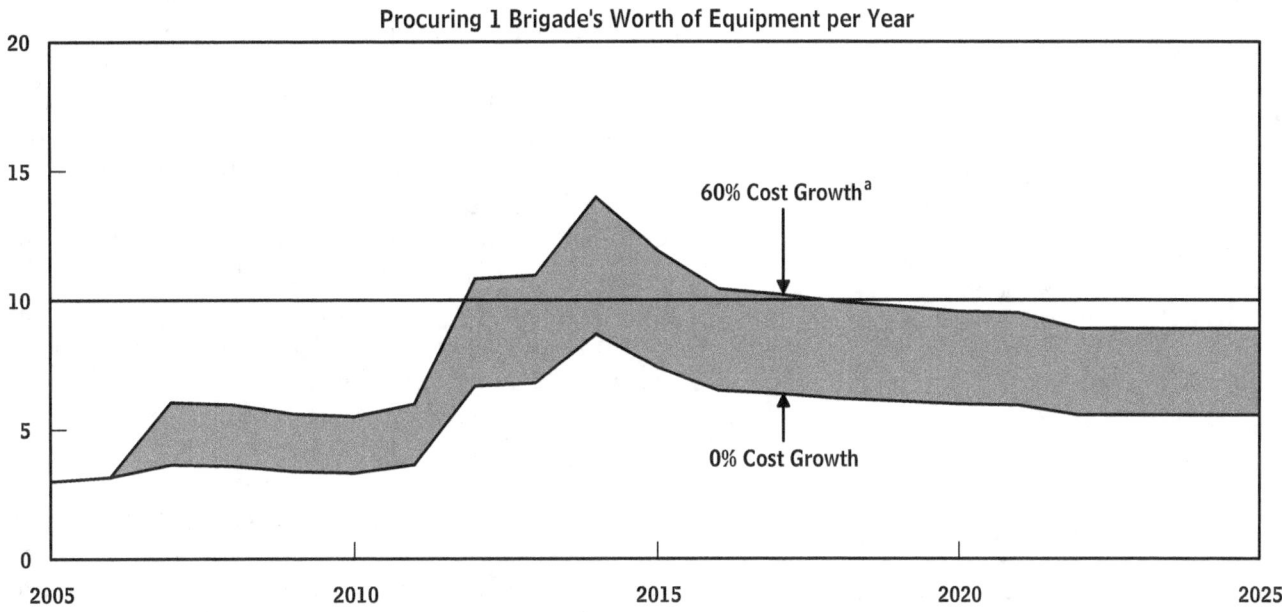

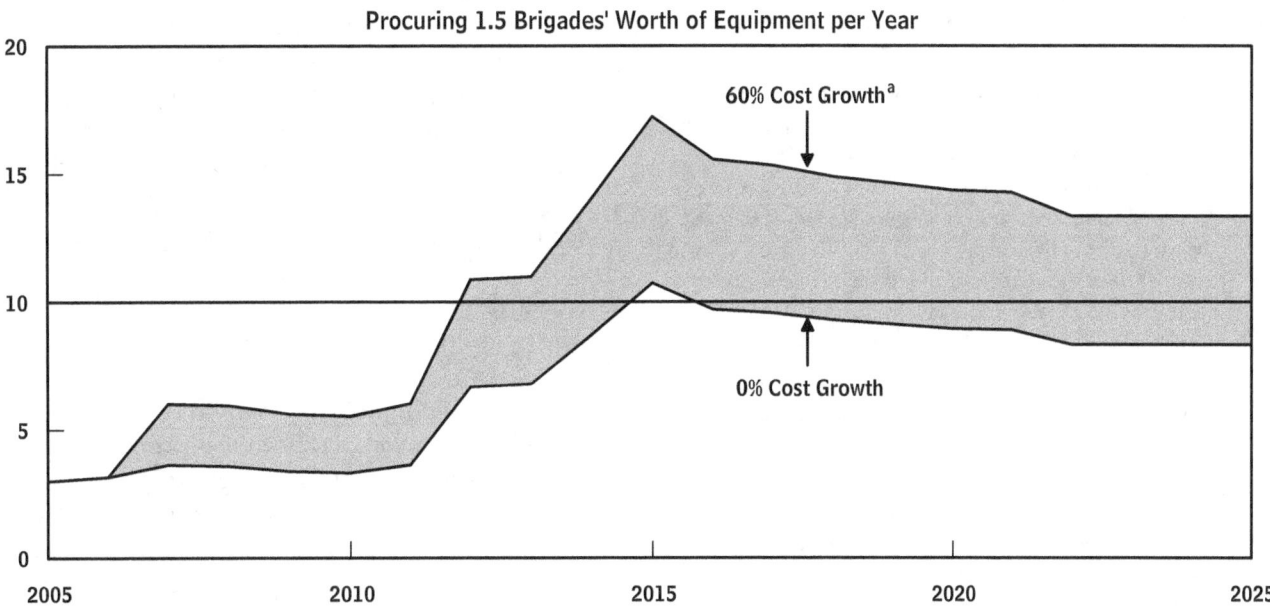

Source: Congressional Budget Office.

Note: Total costs comprise those for research and development and for procurement.

a.   Weighted average of the historical rates of cost growth that apply to the various systems being developed in the FCS program.

Figure 3-8.

Average Age of the Active Armored Combat Vehicle Fleet Under the Administration's Plan with Additional Upgrades

(Average age in years)

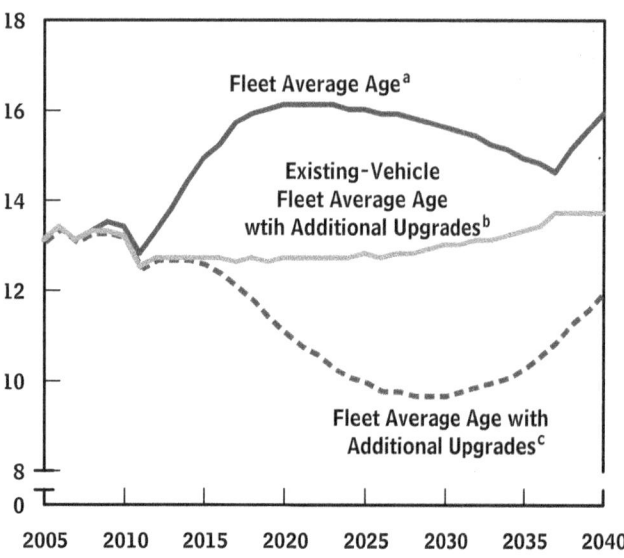

Source: Congressional Budget Office based on data from the Department of the Army.

Note: The "active fleet" comprises all models of the vehicles that CBO estimates will be needed to equip and support modular units in both the Army's active component and the Army National Guard. (Modular units are those resulting from the Army's ongoing modularity initiative, which seeks to make the service more flexible by changing its structure from one based on 18 divisions, several of unique design, to one based on 70 combat brigades, each one of only three designs.)

a.   Includes the effects of introducing Future Combat Systems components into units as well as upgrades to existing systems based on documents submitted with the President's 2007 budget.

b.   Includes the effects of upgrades to existing systems based on documents submitted with the President's 2007 budget and upgrades to Abrams tanks, Bradley fighting vehicles, M113-based vehicles, and M109 howitzers to maintain a relatively constant average age for each fleet of vehicles after 2011.

c.   Includes the effects of introducing FCS components into units as well as upgrades to existing systems based on documents submitted with the President's 2007 budget and upgrades to Abrams tanks, Bradley fighting vehicles, M113-based vehicles, and M109 howitzers to maintain a relatively constant average age for each fleet of vehicles after 2011.

components, such a decision would have implications for the average age of the current fleet of armored combat vehicles. Fifteen brigades' worth of FCS components would not be enough to equip all of the Army's heavy combat brigades; at least 12 of them—potentially four in the Army's active component and eight in the National Guard—and five brigade-sized sets of prepositioned equipment would have to retain their Abrams tanks, Bradley fighting vehicles, M109 howitzers, and M113-based vehicles. In fact, roughly 9,000 of those older vehicles might have to be retained indefinitely. If the Army purchased the 15 brigades' worth of components at the rate of one per year, the average age of such a fleet, without additional upgrades to those older vehicles and even in combination with the newer FCS components, would be roughly 30 years in 2040, by CBO's estimates (see Figure 3-9). Moreover, by 2040, the FCS vehicles purchased to equip the first brigades would be more than 20 years old.

If, for example, the Army bought only 15 brigades' worth of FCS components at the rate of one brigade's worth per year, it would need to invest considerable sums—roughly $25 billion through 2025—to upgrade the large number of vehicles that it planned to retain for some years in order to keep the average age of those systems relatively constant after 2011. (That investment would be about $4 billion more than would be needed if the Army bought FCS components at the rate of 1.5 brigades' worth per year.) The need for more upgrades and therefore more funds would persist through 2040. Furthermore, if the Army purchased only 15 brigades' worth of FCS equipment, it would need to invest roughly $1 billion annually to upgrade the armored vehicles that would remain in its inventory indefinitely.

Survivability of Manned FCS Vehicles

Several observers have questioned the basic assumption that underlies the survivability of lightweight manned FCS vehicles.[22] Supporters of the program claim that knowledge of an enemy's whereabouts—gained through the information sharing made possible by the FCS network—will allow FCS vehicles to avoid unexpected or disadvantageous encounters. In that way, they argue, the

---

22. See Richard Hart Sinnreich, "FCS Needs More Than Just Additional Technical Work," *Lawton (OK) Constitution* (July 25, 2004); "A Science-Fiction Army" (editorial), *New York Times* (March 31, 2005); and Scott Boston, "Toward a Protected Future Force," *Parameters* (Winter 2004-2005), p. 55.

Figure 3-9.

Average Age and Composition of the Active Armored Combat Vehicle Fleet with Limited Purchases of FCS Components

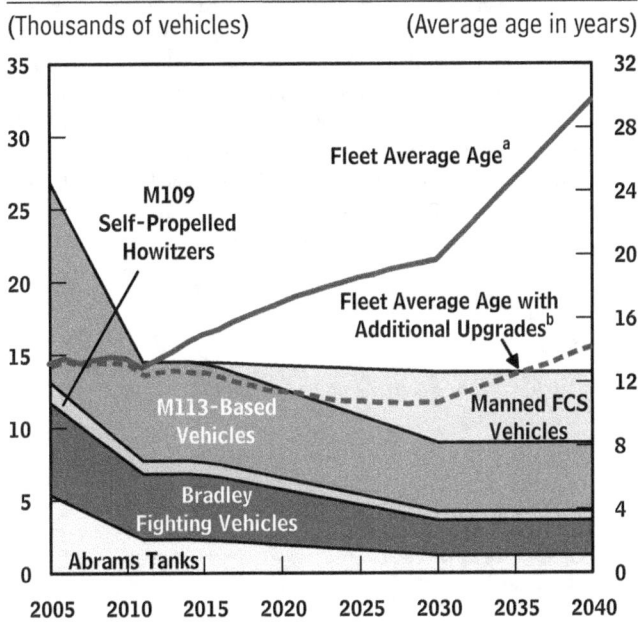

(Thousands of vehicles)   (Average age in years)

Source: Congressional Budget Office based on data from the Department of the Army.

Notes: The "active fleet" comprises all models of the vehicles that CBO estimates will be needed to equip and support modular units in both the Army's active component and the Army National Guard. (Modular units are those resulting from the Army's ongoing modularity initiative, which seeks to make the service more flexible by changing its structure from one based on 18 divisions, several of unique design, to one based on 70 combat brigades, each one of only three designs.)

FCS = Future Combat Systems.

a.   Reflects upgrades to existing systems based on documents submitted with the President's 2007 budget.

b.   Includes upgrades to Abrams tanks, Bradley fighting vehicles, M113-based vehicles, and M109 howitzers to maintain a relatively constant average age for each fleet of vehicles after 2011.

more lightly armored manned FCS vehicles will be just as long-lived on the battlefield as their more heavily armored counterparts are today. Some defense analysts, however, have called into question the viability and technical feasibility of a network that would enable each of hundreds—if not thousands—of systems to know its own location with respect to those of its fellow friendly vehicles as well as those of the enemy's. Without that knowledge and the resultant ability to avoid unfavorable encounters with adversaries, the survivability of lightly armored FCS vehicles might be called into question.

Another concern expressed by soldiers and commanders who have returned from Iraq is whether FCS-type sensors will be able to detect and locate suicide bombers and car bombs, which have proven to be the greatest threat that U.S. forces are facing in Iraq.[23] As a consequence, they argue, the sensors and network that are part of the FCS program will not be able to make FCS vehicles survivable, and because contacts with the enemy will be inevitable, greater protection, such as that provided by current armored vehicles, is necessary.

Congressional Concerns

Members of the House Appropriations and Armed Services Committees, reflecting their doubts about the technical maturity of the components of the FCS program, did not provide all of the funding for it that the Administration requested for 2006. Authorizers specifically targeted manned ground vehicles and blocked funding for them until "mature technologies have been demonstrated in a relevant environment" and proved capable of providing lethality and survivability at least equal to those of the

23. Joshua Kucera, "Iraq Conflict Raises Doubts on FCS Survivability," *Jane's Defense Weekly* (May 19, 2004), p. 8; and statement of Congressman Neil Abercrombie at a hearing before the Subcommittee on Tactical Air and Land Forces of the House Armed Services Committee, "Fiscal Year 2007 Budget Request for Future Combat Systems, Modularity, and Force Protection Initiatives," April 4, 2006.

Army's current fleet of vehicles.[24] In addition, appropriators and authorizers questioned whether sufficient funding would be available in coming years to afford both the FCS program and the Army's modularity initiative.[25] Those concerns, as well as the immaturity of needed technologies, the instability of the program's schedule, and the lack of an independent cost estimate, have caused

some Members of Congress to question the large sums of money that the Army plans to devote to the FCS program and have prompted a search for potential alternatives, some of which are discussed in the next chapter.[26]

---

24. House Armed Services Committee, *National Defense Authorization Act for Fiscal Year 2006*, Report 109-89 (May 20, 2005), p. 257.

25. House Appropriations Committee, *Department of Defense Appropriation Bill, 2006*, Report 109-119 (June 10, 2005), p. 231; and statement of Congressman Neil Abercrombie, April 4, 2006.

26. Congressman Neil Abercrombie, as reported in *Inside the Army*, "Authorizers Differ Over Funding for Future Combat System Program," May 16, 2005; Congressman Curt Weldon, as reported in *Inside the Army*, "Congress May Consider Changes to FCS in Authorization Bill," May 9, 2005; and opening statement of Chairman Curt Weldon at a hearing before the Subcommittee on Tactical Air and Land Forces of the House Armed Services Committee, "Fiscal Year 2007 Budget Request for Future Combat Systems, Modularity, and Force Protection Initiatives," April 4, 2006.

CHAPTER 4

Alternative Approaches to Modernizing the Army's Heavy Forces

The Congressional Budget Office analyzed four options for modernizing the Army's armored units that would address concerns about the Future Combat Systems program, including its technical feasibility and affordability as it is currently structured and the slow rate of introduction of FCS components into the Army's force structure. Three of the alternatives that CBO examined would retain various portions of the FCS program while canceling the remainder. The fourth alternative would cancel development and procurement of the program's new weapon systems but retain the FCS network and associated software and integration elements.

The three options that would retain significant portions of the FCS program—Alternatives 1 through 3—were structured to emphasize systems that would contribute to different capabilities (see Table 4-1). Under the first alternative, the Army would develop and purchase the full suite of sensors called for in the FCS program—the unattended ground sensors and all four classes of unmanned aerial vehicles, together with the network—to enhance units' ability to collect and disseminate information. The second alternative, in addition to the network, would emphasize FCS components that could improve the Army's ability to carry out long-range strikes; under that option, the Army would develop and purchase the unattended ground sensors and longer-range UAVs (Classes III and IV) for detecting and tracking targets and the non-line-of-sight launch system for attacking them. Under the third alternative, the Army would focus on enhancing the maneuvering ability of its brigades by developing several of the manned FCS ground vehicles (particularly those that would replace the older M113-based vehicles and M109 self-propelled howitzers now in the combat vehicle fleet) and the network to tie them together. Under the fourth alternative, the Army would develop only the network and forgo acquisition of any other FCS compo-

nents. Under none of the alternatives would the service develop or procure the unmanned ground vehicles or intelligent munitions systems that are currently planned for the FCS program.

Under all four alternatives, however, the Army would upgrade existing armored vehicles to convert them to the latest models and prevent their average age from rising. Those modernization efforts would also integrate any capabilities gained from the various FCS components that were retained—that is, when those systems became available.

CBO evaluated each of the alternatives on three dimensions: cost, effect on the Army's armored fleet, and effect on the speed of deployment of heavy units. In assessing costs, CBO estimated the total funds needed during the 2007–2025 period to develop and purchase the systems included under each alternative. (Appendix D discusses CBO's cost-estimating methods.) To discern how procuring large numbers of FCS vehicles would affect the armored combat vehicle fleet, CBO evaluated the impact of that procurement in terms of inventory and average age from 2007 through 2040. Effects on deployment speed were measured by calculating the time needed under the various alternatives to deploy brigade- and division-sized units by air and by sea from Savannah, Georgia, to the East African nation of Djibouti.

Alternative 1. Develop and Procure FCS Components That Will Collect and Disseminate Information

Under the first alternative that CBO assessed, the Army would retain only those portions of the FCS program that enhanced its ability to collect information about the location of potential threats and to disseminate that in-

Table 4-1.

Alternatives to the Administration's Current Plan for the FCS Program

Alternative	Emphasis	FCS Components	
		Retained	Canceled
Alternative 1	Collection and sharing of information	Scaled-down network All classes of UAVs Unattended ground sensors	All manned vehicles All unmanned ground vehicles Non-line-of-sight launch system Intelligent munitions system
Alternative 2	Long-range strikes	Scaled-down network UAV Classes III and IV Unattended ground sensors Non-line-of-sight launch system	All manned vehicles UAV Classes I and II All unmanned ground vehicles Intelligent munitions system
Alternative 3	New vehicular technology	Scaled-down network Manned vehicles 　Medical 　Infantry carrier[a] 　Non-line-of-sight mortar 　Non-line-of-sight cannon 　Command and control	All unmanned ground vehicles Manned vehicles 　Mounted combat system 　Recovery and maintenance 　Reconnaissance and surveillance All classes of UAVs Non-line-of-sight launch system Unattended ground sensors Intelligent munitions system
Alternative 4	Network integration with existing systems	Scaled-down network	All manned vehicles All unmanned ground vehicles All classes of UAVs Unattended ground sensors Non-line-of-sight launch system Intelligent munitions system

Source: Congressional Budget Office.

Note: FCS = Future Combat Systems; UAV = unmanned aerial vehicle.

a.   Under Alternative 3, the Army would buy roughly 25 percent of the infantry carrier vehicles included in the Administration's plan.

formation to its combat brigades. As noted earlier, some people argue that if Army units knew more about the location and character of potential threats and the whereabouts of friendly forces, they would be better able to respond and act appropriately, either individually or in concert. To collect as much information as possible, the Army under this alternative would continue to develop and procure the unattended ground sensors and all four classes of UAVs (see Table 4-2). It would also retain the network portion of the FCS program and upgrade its existing armored vehicles to allow them to be integrated into it. All other FCS components, including the manned

and unmanned ground vehicles, the NLOS launch system, and the intelligent munitions system would be canceled.

By greatly increasing the number and types of sensors deployed with a combat brigade, this alternative could significantly enhance the information available to soldiers and commanders in the field about the location of enemy units, friendly forces, civilians, and features of the terrain—as well as about events as they unfolded. In particular:

Table 4-2.

Procurement of FCS Components Under the Administration's Plan and Under Alternative 1

		Components To Be Procured	
Spiral[a]	Fielding to Units Starts	Administration's Plan	Alternative 1
1	2010	Non-line-of-sight launch system Unattended ground sensors Intelligent munitions system Spiral 1 network	Unattended ground sensors Spiral 1 network
2	2012	UAV Class III Spiral 2 network improvements	UAV Class III Spiral 2 network improvements
3	2014	Unmanned ground vehicles Spiral 3 network improvements	UAV Classes I, II, and IV
4	2016	UAV Classes I, II, and IV Manned vehicles Complete network	None

Source: Congressional Budget Office.

Notes: Under Alternative 1, the Army would emphasize the collection and sharing of information.

FCS = Future Combat Systems; UAV = unmanned aerial vehicle.

a.   A spiral is the Army's term for a planned introduction (into units in the field or current systems or both) of technology developed as part of a larger program.

■ The smallest Class I UAVs, which are designed to be operated by one- or two-person teams, could allow individual soldiers to scout nearby terrain, even in an urban setting. In addition, under this alternative, the Army would increase the number of aerial vehicles assigned to a brigade by a factor of five and the number of stations for launching and controlling them by a factor of more than eight. (Today's fully equipped modular heavy combat brigade has four medium-range Shadow UAVs with only one control station and 36 small Raven UAVs with 12 control stations.) The Army would also slightly extend the range of its UAV coverage, boosting it from roughly 50 kilometers (the range of the current Shadow UAV) to 75 km (the range planned for the largest Class IV UAV).

■ The unattended ground sensors, when widely dispersed, could provide remote early warning of any intruders on the ground or in the air over an area of up to 1 square kilometer.

■ A version of the FCS network that would be developed and procured as part of this alternative and integrated into existing combat vehicles would allow the information collected by the numerous sensors to be disseminated and shared by all members of the brigade.

The UAVs and unattended ground sensors are among the least technologically challenging and least expensive of the proposed FCS components. As a result, under this alternative, procurement of some of those components would start earlier than under the Administration's plan: ground sensors and portions of the network in 2008, Class III UAVs in 2010, and the remaining UAVs in 2012.[1] To speed the introduction of FCS technologies into its brigades, the Army would procure components at the rate of three brigades' worth per year—twice the purchase rate that the Administration is planning. Thus, under this alternative, the Army by 2025 would have purchased 33 brigades' worth of Class I, II, and IV UAVs,

---

1.   CBO assumed that components would be introduced into units two years after they were procured.

39 brigades' worth of Class III UAVs, and 45 brigades' worth of unattended ground sensors and the network—enough, in the case of the ground sensors and a rudimentary version of the network, to equip the Army's entire active component plus three additional brigades in the Army National Guard.

To operate effectively with the new FCS components and network and to keep the average age of each fleet of vehicles from increasing after 2011, the armored vehicles that now equip the Army's combat brigades would have to be upgraded. CBO estimates that roughly 80 Abrams tanks, 210 Bradley fighting vehicles, 230 M113-based vehicles, and 40 M109 self-propelled howitzers would need to be upgraded annually for the foreseeable future.

Costs Under Alternative 1

Under this option, the Army would spend a total of $99 billion (excluding any cost growth that might occur) from 2007 through 2025—a substantially smaller amount than the estimate of costs ($140 billion) for the entire FCS program (without upgrades) for the same period. According to CBO's calculations, the cost of the FCS components developed and purchased under this alternative would be $61 billion ($15 billion for research and development and $46 billion for procurement), and the total cost of upgrading the existing armored combat vehicle fleet from 2007 through 2025, including the cost for research and development, would be $38 billion (see Table 4-3). The annual cost of implementing the alternative would be just under $6 billion after 2015—which would be less than the annual cost of the complete FCS program ($8 billion to $10 billion) and represent even greater savings when compared with the annual costs of the program plus upgrades to existing systems ($8 billion to $12 billion; see Figure 4-1 on page 52).[2]

The potential for cost growth under Alternative 1 would probably be less than that under the Administration's

plan during the 2007-2025 period because the Army would be developing and purchasing types of systems that historically have experienced relatively low rates of such growth. Specifically, total costs under this alternative might grow by slightly more than 30 percent—from $99 billion to $131 billion—as a result of increases in the acquisition cost of the UAVs, the network, and the unattended ground sensors. By contrast, the cost of the FCS program as a whole could grow by roughly 60 percent from 2007 through 2025, the result of developing and procuring large numbers of ground vehicles under the Administration's plan, an element that is not part of Alternative 1.

Effect of Alternative 1 on Deployment of Army Units

Because under this alternative the Army would retain the armored combat vehicles that are now in its heavy units, the speed of deployment of such units would be little affected. However, the weight of a modular heavy brigade and associated division would increase because of the additional vehicles needed to support and transport the large number of UAVs that would be added to each brigade.

Currently, modular heavy brigades are equipped with a small number of UAVs similar to the Class III UAV planned for the FCS program and larger numbers of smaller UAVs similar to the FCS Class I UAV. According to the Army's standard equipment tables, each of its modular brigades should be equipped with one Shadow UAV system, which includes four aircraft and a launch and control station supported by generators, communications equipment, and five high-mobility multipurpose wheeled vehicles for transport.[3] Modular heavy brigades are also equipped with 12 Raven systems, each with three aerial vehicles. Those aircraft are much smaller than the Shadow UAVs—they weigh only four pounds—and can be launched by hand. Since they are so small, there are no vehicles in the brigade dedicated to their transport.

Under the structure that the Army is now proposing, an FCS-equipped brigade would have many more UAVs and several more trucks to support them than does a modular

---

2. An even cheaper alternative would be to purchase the unattended ground sensors, UAVs, and network components included under this alternative at the same rate as that planned for the Administration's FCS program. At that rate—1.5 brigades' worth of equipment per year—the total cost of Alternative 1 from 2007 through 2025 would drop to $78 billion, and annual costs after 2015 would be just under $4 billion. However, at that low rate, as under the Administration's plan, a smaller number of brigades—18 to 24—could be equipped with the components purchased through 2025.

3. Based on Office of the Secretary of Defense, *Unmanned Aircraft Systems Roadmap 2005-2030* (August 4, 2005), p. 67, and data from the Department of the Army.

Table 4-3.

Total Acquisition Costs from 2007 to 2025 for the Administration's Plan and Alternatives

(Billions of 2006 dollars)

	Research and Development	Procurement	Total Acquisition
	Administration's Plan		
Costs Included in the President's Budget			
FCS Program's Increment 1[a]	21	101	122
Upgrades to existing vehicles	0	6	6
Further Costs as Estimated by CBO			
Continued purchases of FCS components, 2023 to 2025	0	18	18
Additional upgrades to existing vehicles[b]	2	15	17
Total	**23**	**139**	**162**
	Alternative 1. Collection and Sharing of Information		
FCS Components[c]	15	46	61
Upgrades to Current Systems[b]	2	36	38
Total	**17**	**82**	**99**
	Alternative 2. Long-Range Strikes		
FCS Components[d]	15	52	67
Upgrades to Current Systems[b]	2	36	38
Total	**17**	**89**	**106**
	Alternative 3. New Vehicular Technology		
FCS Components[e]	16	52	67
Upgrades to Current Systems[b]	2	33	35
Total	**18**	**85**	**103**
	Alternative 4. Existing-System Upgrades		
FCS Network	14	16	30
Upgrades to Current Systems[b]	2	36	38
Total	**16**	**52**	**68**

Source: Congressional Budget Office based on data from the Department of the Army.

Notes: The estimated costs presented in this table do not take into account the possibility that costs may grow as they have in similar defense programs in the past.

FCS = Future Combat Systems.

a. Includes costs to develop and purchase 15 brigades' worth of FCS components—enough to equip slightly more than half of the Army's planned 27 heavy brigades (19 brigades in the active Army and eight brigades in the Army National Guard).

b. Includes upgrades to Abrams tanks, Bradley fighting vehicles, M113-based vehicles, and M109 self-propelled howitzers to maintain a relatively constant average age for each fleet of vehicles after 2011.

c. Includes unattended ground sensors, unmanned aerial vehicles (Classes I, II, III, and IV), and the network.

d. Includes unattended ground sensors, unmanned aerial vehicles (Classes III and IV), the non-line-of-sight launch system, and the network.

e. Includes manned vehicles (command and control, medical, non-line-of-sight mortar, non-line-of-sight cannon, and infantry carrier) and the network.

Figure 4-1.

Annual Costs of the Administration's Plan for the Future Combat Systems Program and Alternatives

(Billions of 2006 dollars)

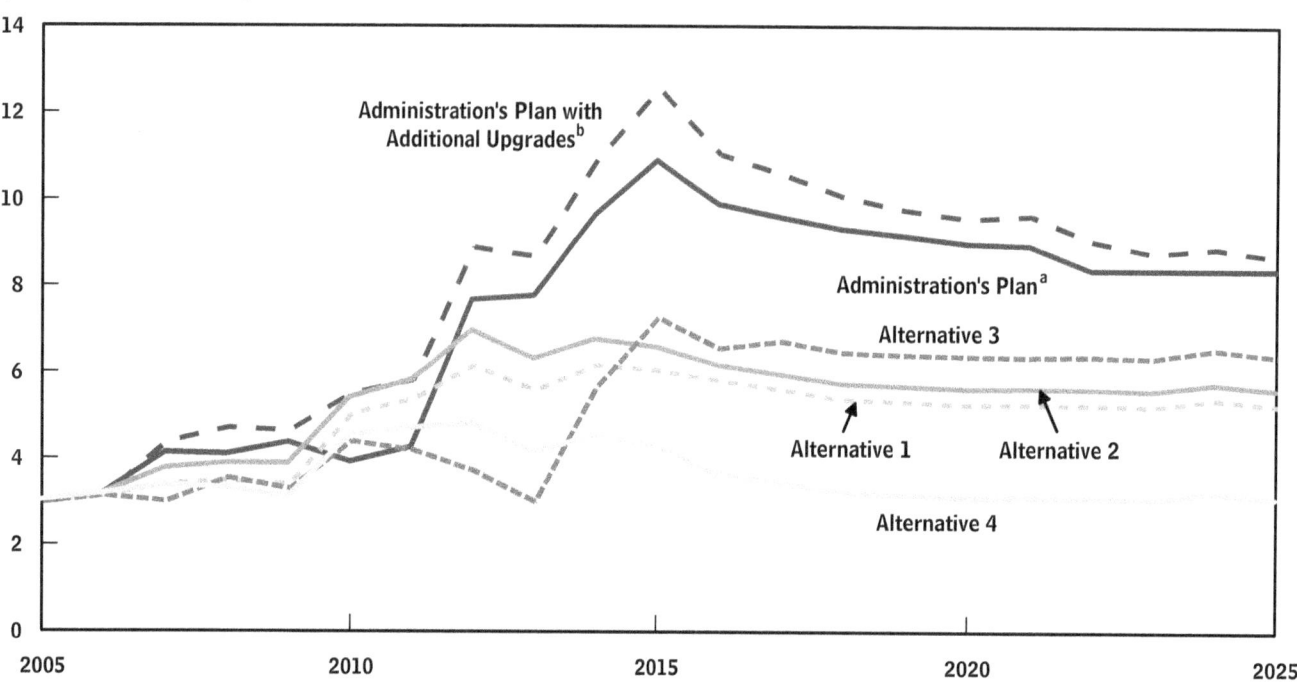

Source: Congressional Budget Office.

Note: See Table 4-1 for a description of the alternatives.

a.   Based on documents submitted with the President's 2007 budget, which includes $6 billion for upgrades to existing systems.

b.   Includes upgrades to Abrams tanks, Bradley fighting vehicles, M113-based vehicles, and M109 howitzers to maintain a relatively constant average age for each fleet of vehicles after 2011.

combat brigade equipped with existing systems.[4] Although, as with the current Raven system, the Army does not plan to dedicate trucks in a combat brigade specifically to transport the new smaller (Classes I and II) UAVs that would be assigned to the unit, the larger FCS Class III and Class IV UAVs would require considerable support. Specifically, each combat brigade is scheduled to include 50 small trucks (HMMWVs) and 12 large trucks (heavy expanded-mobility tactical trucks, or HEMTTs) to transport and support them.

The additional vehicles needed to support the FCS UAVs would represent only a small increase in the weight of a heavy combat brigade. When added to the almost 500 HMMWVs and 135 HEMTTs that are now part of a modular heavy brigade's standard equipment, implementing this alternative might boost the total weight of such a brigade by roughly 500 tons (out of a total 25,000 tons) and add 8,000 square feet to the brigade's total coverage (approximately 320,000 square feet)—for relative increases of less than 3 percent.

Those small increases would have only a limited effect on the time needed to deploy heavy combat units from the continental United States to, for example, Djibouti. Moving a heavy brigade by air that was equipped with the enhanced sensors to be purchased under this alternative might take 10 more C-17 sorties—or an additional half day—to deploy to Djibouti, versus 23 days for a modular

---

4.   Based on data from the Department of the Army and on the fielding plan included in Logistics Requirements and Readiness IPT, Materiel Fielding Sub-IPT, of the Boeing/SAIC Lead Systems Integrator, *Future Combat Systems (FCS) Equipped Unit of Action (UA) Materiel Fielding Plan (MFP) to the UA Supportability Strategy* (April 2005).

Table 4-4.

Time Needed to Deploy Equipment of Combat Units to East Africa

(Days)

	Airlift[a]	Sealift
Brigade-Sized Units		
Administration's Plan[b]		
Modular heavy brigade with existing armored vehicles[c]	23	25
FCS-equipped brigade	18-20	25
Alternatives		
1. Information collection and sharing	23	25
2. Long-range strikes	24	25
3. New vehicular technology	24	25
Division-Sized Units[d]		
Administration's Plan[b]		
Four modular heavy brigades with existing armored vehicles[c]	135	27
Four FCS-equipped brigades	115-130	27
Alternatives		
1. Information collection and sharing	140	27
2. Long-range strikes	140	27
3. New vehicular technology	145	27

Source: Congressional Budget Office based on data from the Department of the Army; Military Traffic Management Command Transportation Engineering Agency, *Deployment Planning Guide: Transportation Assets Required for Deployment*, MTMCTEA Pamphlet 700-5 (May 2001); and Department of the Air Force, *Air Mobility Planning Factors*, Pamphlet 10-1403 (December 18, 2003).

Note: Units would be moved from the continental United States. The data do not reflect the time needed to move sustaining units or supplies. See the text for more discussion of alternatives.

a.   The number of daily sorties constrained by the capacity of the airfield in East Africa, based on average airlift payloads per brigade of 60 tons for modular heavy units and 50 tons to 55 tons for units equipped with Future Combat Systems.

b.   Based on documents submitted with the President's 2007 budget.

c.   "Modular" refers to the Army's ongoing modularity initiative, which seeks to make the service more flexible by changing its structure from one based on 18 divisions, several of unique design, to one based on 70 combat brigades, each one of only three designs. "Heavy" units are those equipped with armored vehicles.

d.   Besides combat brigades, divisions include headquarters and other support units.

heavy brigade with current equipment. The small increase in the total number of vehicles would have no effect on the time to deploy by sea because additional vehicles and supporting gear could fit easily on the ships needed to move a modular heavy brigade with existing equipment overseas (see Table 4-4). For the same reason, the additional vehicles and gear would not affect the time needed to deploy a division-sized unit by sea.

Effect of Alternative 1 on the Current Active Fleet of Armored Combat Vehicles

This alternative would have little effect on the Army's armored combat vehicle fleet. The composition and size of the fleet would remain unchanged: in 2040 as in 2011, the active fleet would comprise roughly 14,500 Abrams tanks, Bradley fighting vehicles, M113-based vehicles, and M109 howitzers (see Figure 4-2). In addition, the fleet's average age would remain relatively constant at about 13 years, because the Army would invest $38 billion in upgrades from 2007 through 2025. By contrast, under the Administration's plan, the average age of the active armored combat vehicle fleet would increase to roughly 16 years in 2020 and then eventually decline, as FCS vehicles replaced significant numbers of the older Abrams tanks, Bradley fighting vehicles, M113-based vehicles, and M109 howitzers.

Advantages and Disadvantages of Alternative 1

The major advantage of Alternative 1 is that under it, the Army would introduce new technology into its units more rapidly than under the Administration's plan and at a lower cost. Because the Army would be developing and fielding some of the least technologically risky and least expensive of the FCS components (UAVs and unattended ground sensors), it could begin to introduce them into units in 2010 and purchase them at rates twice as high (three brigades' worth of equipment per year) as the Administration's planned annual purchases (1.5 brigades' worth). As a result, by 2025, the Army under this alternative would have purchased enough Class III UAVs and network systems for 45 brigades—enough to equip all of the brigades in the Army's active component plus three brigades in the National Guard, or enough to equip all of the Army's heavy brigades (including five brigades' worth of prepositioned stocks) plus 13 additional infantry or Stryker brigades. Costs under this alternative would be less than under the Administration's plan, and the potential for cost growth would be half as great.

Figure 4-2.

Average Age and Composition of the Active Armored Combat Vehicle Fleet Under All Alternatives

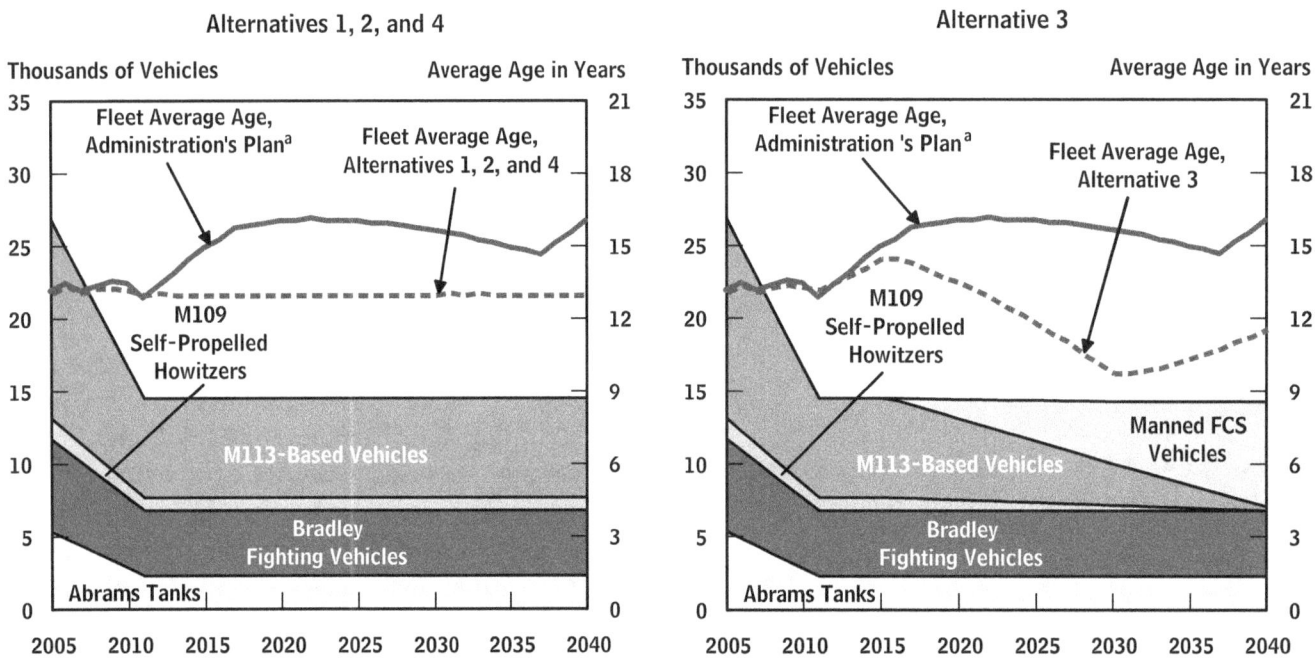

Source: Congressional Budget Office.

Note: See Table 4-1 for a description of the alternatives. FCS = Future Combat Systems.

a.   Reflects upgrades to existing systems based on documents submitted with the President's 2007 budget.

Of course, this option would also suffer from disadvantages when compared with the Administration's plan. Under Alternative 1, the Army would retain its current fleet of armored combat vehicles indefinitely. And even though it would invest $38 billion to upgrade them, by 2040, some of those vehicles would have been in the Army's inventory for almost 60 years. Another disadvantage is the technical risk involved in introducing network technology and associated communications links into older systems, such as the Abrams tanks and Bradley fighting vehicles. Previous attempts to upgrade the electronics suites in those vehicles, including communications and data-processing equipment, have met with some difficulties. In addition, because the Army would retain its older and more bulky armored vehicles, its heavy units would be slightly more difficult to deploy overseas than would units equipped solely with FCS vehicles—although, as mentioned earlier, that difference might not be practically significant.

Alternative 2. Develop and Procure FCS Components That Will Enhance the Army's Long-Range Strike Capability

Under the second alternative to the current FCS program, the Army would retain components that would enhance its ability to carry out long-range strikes—specifically, the unattended ground sensors and the two long-range classes of UAVs (Classes III and IV) to detect and track targets, and the NLOS launch system and its associated missiles to attack those targets (see Table 4-5). All of the ground vehicles in the FCS program, both manned and unmanned, would be canceled under this alternative, as would the shorter-range UAVs (Classes I and II) and the intelligent munitions system. The Army would retain and upgrade its current fleet of armored combat vehicles; it would also develop and procure the FCS network to tie the sensors, launchers, and manned vehicles together.

Developing and fielding the NLOS launch system and long-range UAVs would extend a brigade's ability to detect and strike targets at ranges that exceed its current

Table 4-5.

Procurement of FCS Components Under the Administration's Plan and Under Alternative 2

Spiral[a]	Fielding to Units Starts	Components To Be Procured	
		Administration's Plan	Alternative 2
1	2010	Non-line-of-sight launch system Unattended ground sensors Intelligent munitions system Spiral 1 network	Non-line-of-sight launch system Unattended ground sensors Spiral 1 network
2	2012	UAV Class III Spiral 2 network improvements	UAV Class III Spiral 2 network improvements
3	2014	Unmanned ground vehicles Spiral 3 network improvements	UAV Class IV
4	2016	UAV Classes I, II, and IV Manned vehicles Complete network	None

Source: Congressional Budget Office.

Notes: Under Alternative 2, the Army would emphasize long-range strikes.

FCS = Future Combat Systems; UAV = unmanned aerial vehicles

a. A spiral is the Army's term for a planned introduction (into units in the field or current systems or both) of technology developed as part of a larger program.

capability. (The A6 version of the M109 howitzer is the only existing system assigned to a modular brigade that can attack targets at distances of more than 20 km.) By using long-range Class IV UAVs to detect targets as far away as 75 km and the NLOS launch system to attack them at distances of up to 70 km, a brigade could defeat enemy forces before it was within range of their weapons.

Those same enemy targets could also be attacked by using the Air Force's close-support aircraft or the Army's helicopters, but in some circumstances, such support might not be available quickly enough. For example, bad weather might prevent aircraft from flying, or the Air Force might have higher priorities that would send its aircraft off to carry out a different mission. Similarly, helicopters might be kept on the ground because of unfavorable conditions, such as bad weather or sandstorms. (Or they, too, might be busy elsewhere with higher-priority missions.) Moreover, should a unit suddenly come under attack from long-range enemy artillery, there might not be time to order a retaliatory attack by fixed-wing aircraft or helicopters before the enemy escaped to a safe location. In such circumstances, on-the-spot targeting from UAVs

and the rapid return of fire by quickly activated NLOS launch systems would offer capabilities that today's brigades lack.

Costs and Procurement Schedule Under Alternative 2

Under this alternative, as under the previous one, the Army would develop and procure some of the least technologically challenging and least expensive FCS components. As a result, rates of procurement could be higher than those planned by the Administration, but the ensuing costs would be lower. Specifically, starting in 2016 and continuing through 2025, the Army each year under this alternative would buy three brigades' worth of unattended ground sensors, Class III and IV UAVs, NLOS launch systems, and network hardware. Procurement of the ground sensors and launch systems, which are the most technologically mature of the FCS components to be bought under this alternative, would start in 2008;[5]

---

5. Procurement of portions of the network associated with the unattended ground sensors and NLOS launch systems would also begin in 2008.

procurement of the Class III UAV, in 2010; and that of the Class IV UAV, in 2012. All told, from 2007 through 2025, the Army would buy 45 brigades' worth of unattended ground sensors, NLOS launch systems, and network hardware; 39 brigades' worth of Class III UAVs; and 33 brigades' worth of Class IV UAVs. Total procurement costs for those systems would be $52 billion; the associated costs to develop them would be $15 billion over the same period.

This alternative, like Alternative 1, would require the retention and upgrading of the armored combat vehicles currently needed to equip and support the modular Army. Costs for those vehicles over the 2007–2025 period would be identical to those under Alternative 1: $2 billion for research and development and $36 billion for procurement. In total, costs under Alternative 2 during that period would equal $106 billion—$7 billion more than under the previous alternative but considerably less than under the Administration's plan (see Table 4-3 on page 51). Annual costs would be roughly $6 billion to $7 billion (see Figure 4-1 on page 52). As was the case under the previous alternative, the potential for cost growth would be much lower (by roughly one-third) for the FCS components included under this alternative than it would be for those associated with the FCS program as a whole, which on the basis of past experience could see a rise in costs of about 60 percent.

Effect of Alternative 2 on Deployment of Army Units

Carrying out this alternative could add some weight to the equipment deployed with the Army's brigades, but it would not significantly affect the time required for deployment. As was the case under the previous alternative, equipping Army brigades with dozens of relatively large UAVs would mean adding more than 60 trucks to a brigade's total inventory. Under this alternative, each brigade would also be equipped with 60 NLOS launch systems—and the 30 large trucks and four HMMWVs needed to support them.

In total, the Army under this option might add about 100 vehicles to each brigade's inventory, which could translate into 1,100 tons of additional weight and 16,000 square feet of additional coverage. Those increases in turn would represent about 20 additional C-17 sorties and an increase of one day in the time needed to deploy by air; for deployment by sea, they would represent about 10 percent of the deck space on a fast sealift ship or 5 percent of that on a large medium-speed roll-on/roll-off ship

but no increase in the time needed to deploy a brigade (see Table 4-4 on page 53). Nor would the Army under this alternative find that it needed more time to deploy a division (composed of four modular heavy brigades equipped with Class III and IV UAVs and NLOS launch systems) by sea compared with the time needed to deploy the same division equipped with existing systems.

Effect of Alternative 2 on the Current Active Fleet of Armored Combat Vehicles

Under this option, the Army's active fleet of armored vehicles would be only minimally affected. Over the 19 years from 2007 through 2025, the Army would invest $38 billion to maintain the average age of its approximately 14,500 armored combat vehicles at a constant 13 years—which is significantly lower than the average age of the fleet that would result under the Administration's plan (see Figure 4-2 on page 54).

Advantages and Disadvantages of Alternative 2

The Army under this option would increase the firepower of its brigades sooner than it would under the Administration's plan, and it would do so at a lower cost. By canceling parts of the FCS program, primarily the high-cost ground vehicles, the Army would save $73 billion from 2007 through 2025 and would be able to buy enough high-volume missile launchers to equip 45 brigades—an increase of 21 brigades over what it could buy under the Administration's plan during the same period.[6] Moreover, under this alternative, the Army's R&D efforts would be less technologically risky and the systems it developed and procured would have a lower potential for cost growth. Finally, by investing $38 billion of the savings realized by canceling portions of the FCS program in upgrades to its existing armored vehicles, the Army could maintain the age of the active fleet at a constant 13 years.

On at least two counts, however, this alternative would not compare favorably with the Administration's plan. First, under this option, the Army's current fleet of armored combat vehicles would be retained indefinitely. Given that those vehicles were originally designed in the 1970s or earlier, it might be difficult to integrate them—using the FCS network—with the FCS sensors and the NLOS launch systems. Second, the weight and bulk of

---

6. That comparison incorporates the assumption that the Administration would continue to purchase 1.5 brigades' worth of FCS components annually through 2025.

the Army's combat brigades would increase because of the additional equipment required under this alternative, with the result that an extra day might be added to the time needed to deploy a brigade by air.

Alternative 3. Emphasize Investment in New Manned Combat Vehicles

Development and procurement of new vehicles to replace many of the Army's oldest combat vehicles would be the main emphasis of Alternative 3. The new vehicles would include most, but not all, of those currently under development in the FCS program—specifically, the FCS command-and-control vehicle, mortar carrier (NLOS-M), medical evacuation and treatment vehicle, infantry carrier, and howitzer (NLOS-C). When fielded in large enough numbers, those vehicles could eventually replace all of the M113-based vehicles and M109 howitzers now assigned to heavy combat brigades. The FCS vehicles would address at least some of the problems (such as the inability of the M109 howitzers to keep up with the newer Abrams tanks and Bradley fighting vehicles) that the Army has said are associated with keeping those older vehicles in its combat units.

Under this alternative, the Army would retain its Abrams tanks and Bradley fighting vehicles and upgrade them rather than replace them with vehicles developed in the FCS program. It would also upgrade M113-based vehicles and M109 howitzers assigned to units outside of combat brigades until those systems could be replaced by FCS vehicles. In addition, the Army would continue to develop the FCS network and install appropriate hardware in the Abrams tanks and Bradley fighting vehicles during upgrades so that they, too, could be integrated into the network (see Table 4-6).

By developing and fielding new vehicles to replace those that have, in one form or another, been in the Army's inventory for more than 40 years, this alternative would greatly enhance the lethality and technological sophistication of a large portion of the armored combat vehicles in the Army's brigades. The FCS vehicles that would replace the M113-based vehicles and M109 howitzers in a heavy brigade would be equipped with better armaments and electronic gear. For example, the NLOS-C, as currently envisioned, would be capable of higher rates of fire than the A6 version of the M109 howitzer and, because of its improved fire-control systems, would be more accurate in its delivery of artillery rounds. Likewise, the NLOS-M,

according to current designs, would be a more lethal weapon than the mortar on the M113-based vehicle, capable of reacting more quickly to threats and firing more mortar rounds per minute.

In addition to the greater lethality that the Army would gain under this alternative, its fielding of the sophisticated medical evacuation vehicle that is part of the FCS program should enhance the survivability of soldiers who are wounded on the battlefield.

Under this alternative, the Army would cancel several portions of the FCS program and reduce others. Specifically, it would:

■ Cancel all programs to develop and procure unmanned systems, including all four classes of UAVs, all unmanned ground vehicles, the NLOS launch system, the unattended ground sensors, and the intelligent munitions system;

■ Cancel manned ground vehicles (the mounted combat system and the reconnaissance and surveillance vehicle) that are slated to perform missions currently assigned to the Abrams tanks and Bradley cavalry fighting vehicles;

■ Reduce by about 75 percent the number of FCS infantry carrier vehicles purchased per brigade to reflect the fact that the Bradley infantry fighting vehicles will be retained in the heavy brigades;

■ Cancel the planned programs for the FCS maintenance and recovery vehicle (because the Abrams tanks would be retained and thus so would the current M88 heavy recovery vehicle); and

■ Scale back procurement of the FCS network, a version of which would be developed and fielded under this alternative, to reflect the smaller number of systems that it would have to support in each brigade.

Because the Army under this alternative would retain the Abrams tanks and Bradley fighting vehicles indefinitely, it would upgrade them sufficiently to prevent their average age from increasing after 2011. However, because the Army would focus on accelerating the fielding of FCS components to replace the M113-based vehicles and M109 howitzers currently in its combat brigades, it

Table 4-6.

Procurement of FCS Components Under the Administration's Plan and Under Alternative 3

		Components To Be Procured	
Spiral[a]	Fielding to Units Starts	Administration's Plan	Alternative 3
1	2010	Non-line-of-sight launch system Unattended ground sensors Intelligent munitions system Spiral 1 network	Spiral 1 network
2	2012	UAV Class III Spiral 2 network improvements	Spiral 2 network improvements
3	2014	Unmanned ground vehicles Spiral 3 network improvements	None
4	2016	Manned vehicles 　Medical 　Infantry carrier 　Non-line-of-sight mortar 　Non-line-of-sight cannon 　Command and control 　Mounted combat system 　Recovery and maintenance 　Reconnaissance and surveillance UAV Classes I, II, and IV Complete Network	Manned vehicles 　Medical 　Infantry carrier[b] 　Non-line-of-sight mortar 　Non-line-of-sight cannon 　Command and control

Source: Congressional Budget Office.

Notes: Under Alternative 3, the Army would emphasize new vehicular technology.

　　　　FCS = Future Combat Systems; UAV = unmanned aerial vehicles.

a.   A spiral is the Army's term for a planned introduction (into units in the field or current systems or both) of technology developed as part of a larger program.

b.   Under Alternative 3, the Army would buy roughly 25 percent of the infantry carrier vehicles included in the Administration's plan.

would maintain and upgrade only those vehicles that were retained (until they could be replaced) in units outside of the combat brigades. It would not invest funds in upgrading M113-based and M109 vehicles assigned to combat brigades—because those vehicles would be the first to be replaced by FCS components.

Costs and Procurement Schedule Under Alternative 3

The cost of implementing this alternative would be similar to that of carrying out Alternatives 1 and 2, requiring a total investment of $103 billion from 2007 through 2025. Of that total, $67 billion would be needed to develop and procure the five variants of manned FCS vehi-

cles. Because the Army under this alternative would pursue only a subset of the FCS components included under the Administration's plan, it would be able to purchase two brigades' worth of the manned FCS vehicles each year beginning in 2015, for a total of 23 brigades' worth by 2025. The cost of upgrading the armored combat vehicles from the current fleet that would be retained under this alternative would total $35 billion from 2007 through 2025, the preponderance of which—$33 billion—would go toward procurement (see Table 4-3 on page 51).

Because the manned vehicles are the most technically challenging of the 18 FCS components, their development would take the longest. Consequently, under this alternative, the Army would not begin to purchase those systems until 2014. The annual funding required to implement this alternative would thus be less than that for the previous two alternatives and for the Administration's plan until 2015 (see Figure 4-1 on page 52). Thereafter, annual funding would be slightly higher, at about $6.5 billion, than under the previous alternatives but still significantly below that required under the Administration's plan. Similarly, because the Army would be developing and procuring ground vehicles—the systems whose costs in the past have exceeded estimates by the greatest degree—the potential for cost growth under Alternative 3, at 55 percent, would be higher than under Alternatives 1 and 2 but lower than under the Administration's plan.

Effect of Alternative 3 on Deployment of Army Units

This alternative would have a slight negative effect on the speed of units' deployment because most of the vehicles being replaced would weigh less than their replacements. Under this approach, the Army, on average, would replace slightly less than half of the armored vehicles in a heavy brigade with manned FCS vehicles, but most of the vehicles that would be displaced—120 out of 136—would be based on the M113 chassis and weigh less than the FCS replacements. That would hold true whether the ultimate weight of the FCS vehicles was 24 tons (the design threshold) or 19 tons (the program's original goal) because M113-based vehicles weigh from 12 tons to 14 tons, or considerably less than any potential manned FCS vehicle. As a result, the combined weight of the combat vehicles in a brigade under this alternative could be as much as 1,400 tons more than that of the combat vehicles in a modular heavy brigade equipped with existing armored vehicles.

An argument might be made that the FCS-equipped brigade as a whole would weigh no more than one of today's modular brigades because the manned FCS components would require fewer support vehicles, such as trucks. But given the equipment that is currently scheduled to be assigned to a brigade equipped entirely with FCS components, a brigade equipped as Alternative 3 specifies would still appear to weigh more than the modular brigade it was meant to replace.[7]

The extra weight of the equipment assigned to heavy combat brigades under this alternative might slightly increase the time to deploy a brigade by air, but the change would be insignificant. Deploying a brigade equipped with a combination of FCS and current armored vehicles to Djibouti by air would take 24 days rather than 23 days—but the time it would take to deploy by sea would remain unchanged, at 25 days (see Table 4-4 on page 53). The time to deploy by sea a division-sized heavy unit equipped with the FCS components included under this alternative would also remain at 27 days. (Deploying a division-sized heavy unit by air is impractical; however, to complete the comparisons, it would take roughly 145 days, in CBO's estimation, to deploy a division with four heavy brigades equipped with FCS components as laid out under this alternative, compared with 135 days for a division with four modular heavy brigades equipped with existing vehicles.)

Effect of Alternative 3 on the Armored Combat Fleet

Under this alternative, the Army would introduce new armored combat vehicles faster than it would under the Administration's plan, which would keep the average age of the active fleet below 15 years through 2040 (see Figure 4-2 on page 54). If this alternative was carried out, the Army would have bought and fielded enough FCS vehicles by 2029 to replace all of the M113-based vehicles and M109 howitzers in the heavy combat brigades. Until then, however, a sizable number of M113-based vehicles would be retained, and their average age would exceed 15 years through 2026. (In 2020, the 5,600 M113-based vehicles in the inventory would have an average age of 18 years.) As a consequence, the average age of the active fleet of armored vehicles under this alternative would peak at slightly more than 14 years in 2016 before starting to decline—an improvement over the fleet's condition under the Administration's plan.

Advantages and Disadvantages of Alternative 3

Alternative 3 is unique among the approaches CBO considered in that it would introduce new vehicular technology into the Army's forces, thus offering the advantage that the service could retire some of its oldest armored vehicles earlier than under any of the other alternatives. The option's costs are on a par with those of Alternatives 1

---

7. The FCS design calls for 550 trucks, compared with 880 for a heavy brigade equipped with today's armored combat vehicles. However, the FCS-equipped brigade would have about 15 percent more large trucks—at 20 tons each—than a modular heavy brigade would have. Consequently, the weight of the supporting vehicles for the two types of brigades might be very similar.

and 2; like them, it is considerably less expensive than the Administration's plan.

Alternative 3, however, also shares some of the disadvantages of those previous options. The Army under this alternative would retain its fleets of Abrams tanks and Bradley fighting vehicles indefinitely and would have to incorporate the technology associated with the FCS network into those vehicles. In addition, the risk of cost growth associated with this alternative, although lower than under the Administration's plan, is higher—at 55 percent—than under the other alternatives.

Alternative 4. Develop a Scaled-Down FCS Network and Integrate It with Existing Systems

The last alternative that CBO examined would preserve only that part of the FCS program involved in developing and supporting the network. The new capability—under this alternative, a scaled-down version of the network currently envisioned for the FCS program—would then be integrated into existing armored vehicles, which would be upgraded to keep them current. All other portions of the FCS program would be canceled.

This alternative has the appeal of taking an evolutionary approach to improving the capability of the armored vehicles in the Army's combat brigades rather than providing a wholesale makeover based on unproven technology. By introducing into existing vehicles those portions of the networking improvements that are developed—and proved effective—in the FCS program, the Army under this alternative could take advantage of advances in technology and information sharing yet retain the best features of its current fleet (in particular, the high degree of survivability of the Abrams tank). Those features are not insignificant: through numerous upgrades and the introduction of new technology as it has evolved, the Army's armored combat vehicles have proved to be among the most capable—if not the most capable—weapon systems in the world.

Costs and Procurement Schedule Under Alternative 4

Because the Army would purchase the least amount of hardware under this alternative, the option would be the least expensive of the four CBO considered. Its associated total costs of $68 billion would cover developing and

purchasing the hardware for the FCS network ($30 billion) and upgrading existing armored vehicles ($38 billion; see Table 4-3 on page 51). This alternative would also require the smallest amount of annual funding—roughly $3 billion in 2018 and thereafter—despite the fact that three brigades' worth of FCS network hardware would be purchased each year starting in 2012 (see Figure 4-1 on page 52). At that rate of procurement, the Army by 2025 would have purchased equipment for 45 brigades—enough for all of its heavy brigades (including National Guard units), five prepositioned brigades, and 13 additional combat brigades, either infantry or Stryker. None of the 18 FCS components would be developed or purchased under this alternative. Nevertheless, growth in costs of about 40 percent would still be possible, based on historical experience, because more than half of the alternative's costs would be associated with upgrading existing ground vehicles.

Effect of Alternative 4 on Deployment of Army Units

Because the Army under this alternative would not add any new vehicles to existing combat brigades or replace existing systems with new ones, the ability of its units to deploy overseas would not be affected. The time needed to deploy a heavy brigade to Djibouti by air or by sea would be the same as it is for today's modular heavy brigades—23 days and 25 days, respectively. Similarly, there would be no change in the time needed to move a division-sized unit composed of four modular heavy brigades to Djibouti by sea—which would remain at 27 days.

Effect of Alternative 4 on the Army's Fleet of Armored Vehicles

As it would under Alternatives 1 and 2, the Army under Alternative 4 would retain its existing armored combat vehicles indefinitely. Through upgrades, the average age of the active fleet of roughly 14,500 vehicles could be maintained at about 13 years through 2040. And by 2021, all of those vehicles in heavy brigades could be retrofitted with FCS hardware that would allow them to be integrated into the network—if the Army chose to modernize its heavy brigades first.[8] In any case, the Army's armored combat fleet in 2040 under this alterna-

---

8. Alternatively, with the 45 brigades' worth of network hardware purchased through 2025, the Army could equip all of the brigades in its active component first, followed by three of the prepositioned equipment sets. That approach would leave two prepositioned sets and all 28 National Guard brigades outside the network.

tive would comprise the same vehicles that it did in 2011 (see Figure 4-2 on page 54).

Advantages and Disadvantages of Alternative 4

The greatest advantage of this alternative—the least expensive of the options that CBO examined—is its relatively low estimated cost of $68 billion from 2007 through 2025. Of course, because it would invest so little in new technologies and equipment, it would also offer

the Army the least in terms of innovation. Under this alternative, the service would maintain the same fleet of armored vehicles that it has had for more than 20 years, some of which—notably the M113-based vehicles—have been in service since the Korean War. Although connected by a new network and upgraded to keep them in working condition, those vehicles will offer nothing new to the Army's combat arsenal.

A Description and History of the Army's Current Armored Vehicles

This appendix describes the four types of armored vehicles that make up most of the Army's armored fleet: the M1 Abrams tank, the M2 and M3 Bradley fighting vehicles, vehicles based on the M113 armored personnel carrier, and the M109 self-propelled howitzer. The discussion also touches on the evolution of each of the Army's armored vehicle fleets since the vehicles were first introduced into the Army's inventory.

Abrams Tanks

The Abrams, or M1, tank was developed in the 1970s and initially produced in 1980 with a 105-millimeter (mm) main gun capable of attacking targets up to 3 kilometers (km) away. The primary purpose of the Abrams when it was first introduced was to be able to win in any battle with Soviet tanks. During the 1980s and 1990s, the tank's design underwent changes that were designed to counter the increased capabilities of tanks fielded by the Soviets. Thus, later models of the Abrams tank had a larger 120-mm main gun that was capable of firing shells at higher speeds than the original 105-mm gun. This enabled the later models of the Abrams to attack targets at greater ranges or penetrate thicker armor at the same distance. In addition, the Abrams was given improved heavier armor that enhanced its ability to stop enemy tank rounds (see Table A-1 on page 67). The most recent modifications, known as the System Enhancement Program (SEP) and the Abrams Integrated Management program, were introduced in 1999 and 2000 and included improvements in armor, targeting, communications, and navigation systems.

Not surprisingly, larger guns, heavier armor, and more sensors have added weight to the tank. As a result, the latest version of the Abrams, the M1A2 SEP, weighs more

than 70 tons, compared with the basic M1 model, which weighed roughly 10 tons less (see Table A-1 on page 67).

At the end of 2003, the Army's Abrams fleet of approximately 5,850 tanks contained a mix of models, with the M1A1 accounting for the vast majority (see Figure A-1). And even though the last new tank was delivered to the

Figure A-1.

Average Age and Composition of the Army's A1 Abrams Tank Fleet

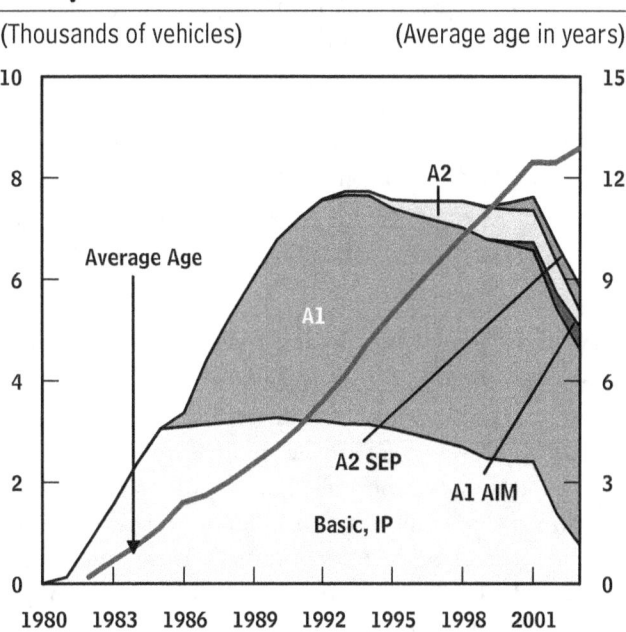

Source: Congressional Budget Office based on data from the Department of the Army.

Notes: The last data points are for the end of 2003.

IP = Improved; AIM = Abrams Integrated Management program; SEP = System Enhancement Program.

Figure A-2.

Average Age and Composition of the Army's M2/M3 Bradley Fighting Vehicle Fleet

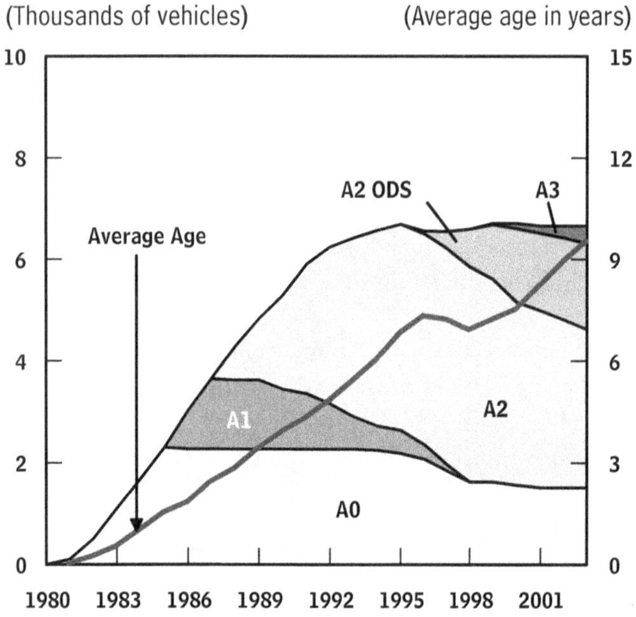

(Thousands of vehicles)   (Average age in years)

Source: Congressional Budget Office based on data from the Department of the Army.

Notes: The last data points are for the end of 2003.

ODS = Operation Desert Storm.

Army in 1993, constant upgrades of existing models and retirement of some older models kept the average age of the tank fleet below 13 years through the end of 2003.

Bradley Fighting Vehicles

The Bradley fighting vehicle was developed in two versions—the infantry (M2) fighting vehicle and the cavalry (M3) fighting vehicle; both are equipped with a 25-mm gun; tube-launched, optically tracked, wire-guided (TOW) antitank missiles; and a 7.62-mm machine gun. The differences between the two versions are minor; because of the kinds of missions it undertakes, the cavalry version carries more radios and missile rounds than does the infantry version, which can carry more soldiers (in addition to the crew of three, six passengers versus two for the cavalry fighting vehicle).

Both versions were introduced in 1981; by the mid-1990s, the Army had purchased roughly 6,700 Bradley fighting vehicles, two-thirds of them in the infantry (M2)

configuration and the remainder in the cavalry (M3) configuration. In terms of the original models of those vehicles (most have been upgraded since they were purchased), the breakdown is as follows:

■ The first 2,300 Bradleys (M2 and M3 combined) purchased from 1981 to 1984 were in the A0, or original, configuration;

■ About 1,400 Bradleys built from 1985 to 1988 were in the A1 design, which incorporated an improved version of the TOW missile system; and

■ The final 3,000 or so Bradleys purchased new were A2 models that included enhanced protection of the crew and passengers, such as additional appliqué steel armor to defend against larger projectiles and an internal liner to prevent hull fragments—or spall—from injuring soldiers inside the vehicle (see Table A-2 on page 68).

Since 1995, the Army has produced very few new Bradley fighting vehicles but instead has been upgrading existing models (see Figure A-2). By 2003, almost 1,700 older versions had been converted to the A2 Operation Desert Storm (A2 ODS) configuration, which features an improved rangefinder and navigation system. The most recent versions of the Bradley fighting vehicle—the M2A3 and M3A3—were introduced in 1999 and include digital communications, improved viewers and sensors, an improved turret drive, and survivability enhancements, such as titanium armor for the roof. As a result of the upgrades that many Bradleys have undergone, the average age of the fleet is considerably lower than the vehicles' original production dates might indicate. (Those dates range from 1980 to 1994.) Indeed, the modernization of more than 2,500 Bradleys since 1995 resulted in an average age for the fleet of 10 years at the end of 2003—rather than an average age closer to 20 years, which would have been expected in the absence of the upgrades (see Figure A-2).

As with the Abrams tank, improvements in the Bradley fighting vehicle's capabilities have made subsequent models heavier. The original A0 model weighed 25 tons, but the additional equipment and improved armor of the later A2 and A3 models added 7 tons and 8 tons, respectively, to the vehicles' total weight. The additional weight reduced the Bradley's fuel efficiency slightly from 1.7 miles per gallon (mpg) for the earliest models to 1.5 mpg and 1.4 mpg for the A2 and A3 models.

Figure A-3.

Average Age and Composition of the Army's M113-Based Vehicle Fleet

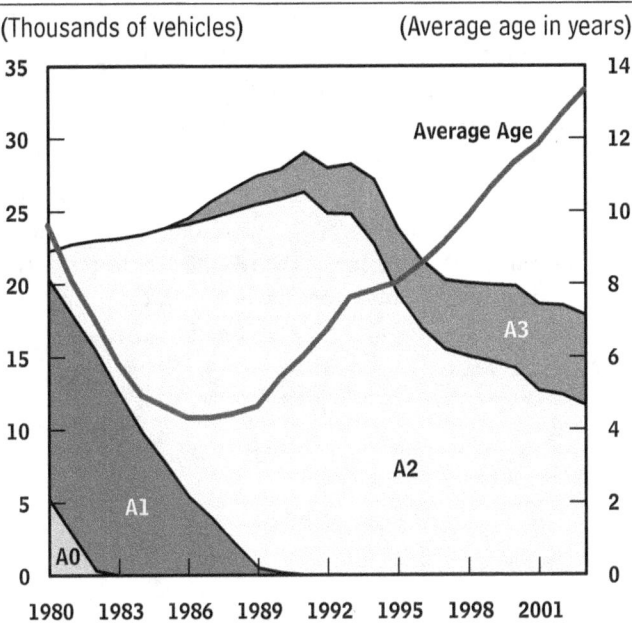

(Thousands of vehicles) (Average age in years)

Source: Congressional Budget Office based on data from the Department of the Army.

Note: The last data points are for the end of 2003.

The M113 Family of Vehicles

The Army began developing the original M113 in 1956 to provide armored and infantry units with a lightweight multipurpose personnel carrier. Designed from the beginning with certain features (for example, to be amphibious and capable of being dropped into a theater by air) but with the ability to adapt to multiple functions, the M113 has been fielded in various configurations, including smoke generator, mortar carrier, cargo carrier, command post, antitank missile carrier, and personnel carrier. The most numerous of the Army's armored vehicles, with roughly 18,000 in service at the end of 2003, the M113 is also the Army's only armored vehicle that weighs less than 20 tons or that has a fuel efficiency that exceeds 2 mpg. Even the largest model of the M113 vehicle is relatively compact and—at 17 feet long, 9 feet wide, and 8 feet tall—is considerably smaller than either the Abrams tank or Bradley fighting vehicles.

Since it was first developed, the M113 vehicle has been modified several times. The first enhancement—the switch from a gasoline engine in the original M113

model to a diesel engine in the M113A1 and subsequent models—came in the 1960s, shortly after the vehicle was first fielded. Then, after producing 18,000 A0 and A1 models in the 1960s and 1970s, the Army embarked on a product improvement program in the 1980s and 1990s that resulted in a totally revamped fleet. The M113A2, introduced in 1979, incorporated enhanced cooling for the engine and improved suspension (see Table A-3 on page 69); that model accounted for roughly two-thirds of the M113 fleet at the end of 2003 (see Figure A-3). The latest variant, the M113A3, was first produced in the mid-1980s and includes an improved transmission and drive train, simpler driver controls, and an antispall liner. Although no new M113A3s have been produced since 1992, by 2003, the Army had converted more than 2,000 older model M113s to the A3 configuration.

The continual upgrading of existing M113s since the late 1970s kept the average age of the fleet below 10 years through 1998 (see Figure A-3). However, the rate of conversions since 1995 has not been sufficient to retard the aging of the fleet, even though large numbers of older vehicles have been retired. As a result, the average age of the roughly 18,000 M113-based vehicles in the Army's inventory at the end of 2003 was slightly greater than 13 years.

M109 Self-Propelled Howitzer

The M109 self-propelled howitzer has been in the Army's inventory of armored vehicles since 1962. Its 155-mm cannon provides supporting fire to the Army's combat units and can shell targets at a distance of 30 km. The latest model of the howitzer weighs more than 30 tons, is the largest of the Army's current fleet of armored vehicles (32 feet long by 10 feet wide by 11 feet high), and has a fuel efficiency of less than 2 mpg (see Table A-4 on page 70).

Like the Army's other armored vehicles that have been in service since the 1960s, the M109 has undergone several upgrades, although all but the most recent have not involved significant modifications. Compared with the original version, subsequent models (A2, A3, A4, and A5) have mounted 155-mm cannons with longer barrels and greater ranges. Additional improvements include air purifiers and heaters for the crew's protection and comfort, an external rack at the back of the turret for carrying equipment, and increased reliability.

Figure A-4.

Average Age and Composition of the Army's Fleet of M109 Self-Propelled Howitzers

(Thousands of vehicles)   (Average age in years)

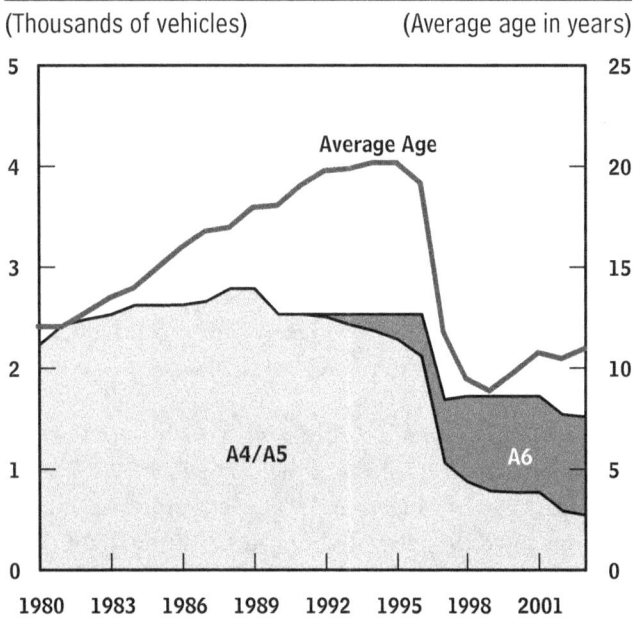

Source: Congressional Budget Office based on data from the Department of the Army.

Note: The last data points are for the end of 2003.

As part of a major upgrade program, the Army began converting existing howitzers to the A6, or Paladin, model in 1991 and by the end of 2003 had a total of 975 M109A6s in its inventory. The improvements provided by that upgrade included supplemental armor and a spall liner; a fire-suppression system; better engine cooling; enhanced suspension, hydraulic, and electrical systems; a new fire-control computer; and a new cannon mount. The extensive modifications involved in the Paladin upgrades—which effectively resulted in a new howitzer—combined with the decommissioning of older models reduced the average age of the M109 fleet to roughly nine years in 1999. Subsequently, however, the average age increased; by the end of 2003, it had reached 11 years (see Figure A-4).

Table A-1.

Characteristics of Models of the Abrams (M1) Tank

	Model					
	Basic	**IP**	**A1**	**A1 AIM**	**A2**	**A2 SEP**
Date of Introduction	1981	1985	1985	2000	1991	1999
Combat Weight (Tons)	60	61	67	68	70	70+
Range (Miles)	280	310	275	275	265	265
Fuel						
Capacity (Gallons)	504	504	504	504	504	504
Efficiency (mpg)	0.6	0.6	0.5	0.5	0.5	0.5
Size of Main Gun (mm)	105	105	120	120	120	120
Vehicle Dimensions (Length x width x height, in feet)	32 x 12 x 9	32 x 12 x 9	32 x 12 x 9	32 x 12 x 9	32 x 12 x 9	32 x 12 x 9
Improvements Over Previous Model						
Armor	n.a.	Improved composite armor	n.a.	Heavy armor added to hull and turret	Second-generation depleted-uranium armor	Third-generation depleted-uranium armor
Other	n.a.	n.a.	Improved suspension Active NBC protective system	Digital electronics	Commander's independent thermal viewer Digital electronics SINCGARS radio	Second-generation FLIR for commander's independent thermal viewer Integrated GPS

Source: Congressional Budget Office based on its February 1993 report *Alternatives for the U.S. Tank Industrial Base;* and Gary W. Cooke, "Gary's Combat Vehicle Reference Guide,"available at www.inetres.com/gp/military/cv/index.html.

Notes: IP = Improved; AIM = Abrams Integrated Management program; SEP = System Enhancement Program; mpg = miles per gallon; mm = millimeters; n.a. = not applicable; NBC = nuclear, biological, chemical; FLIR = forward-looking infrared; GPS = global positioning system; SINCGARS = single-channel ground and airborne radio system.

Table A-2.

Characteristics of Models of the Bradley Infantry (M2) and Cavalry (M3) Fighting Vehicles

	Model				
	A0	A1	A2	A2 ODS	A3
Date of Introduction	1981	1986	1988	1997	1999
Combat Weight (Tons)	25	25	32	32	33
Range (Miles)	300	300	265	265	250
Fuel					
Capacity (Gallons)	175	175	175	175	175
Efficiency (mpg)	1.7	1.7	1.5	1.5	1.4
Dimensions (Length x width x height, in feet)	22 x 11 x 10	22 x 11 x 10	22 x 11 x 10	22 x 11 x 10	22 x 11 x 12
Improvements Over Previous Model					
Armor	n.a.	n.a.	Additional appliqué armor	n.a.	Titanium roof armor
Other	n.a.	Improved suspension Improved TOW missile system NBC filter system	More powerful engine Antispall liner[a]	Laser rangefinder GPS navigation	Digital communications Second-generation FLIR for commander's independent viewer and driver's vision enhancer

Source: Congressional Budget Office based on data from the Department of the Army; Gary W. Cooke, "Gary's Combat Vehicle Reference Guide," available at www.inetres.com/gp/military/cv/index.html; and Christopher Foss, ed., *Jane's Armour and Artillery, 2003–2004* (Alexandria, Va.: Jane's Information Group, 2003).

Note: ODS = Operation Desert Storm; mpg = miles per gallon; n.a. = not applicable; TOW = tube-launched, optically tracked, wire-guided; GPS = global positioning system; NBC = nuclear, biological, chemical; FLIR = forward-looking infrared.

a. The liner protects vehicle occupants from hull fragments.

Table A-3.

Characteristics of Models of the M113-Based Family of Vehicles

	Model			
	A0	**A1**	**A2**	**A3**
Date of Introduction	1961	1964	1979	1986
Combat Weight (Tons)	12	12	12	14
Range (Miles)	300	300	300	300
Fuel				
Capacity (Gallons)	95	95	95	95
Efficiency (mpg)	3.2	3.2	3.2	3.2
Dimensions (Length x width x height, in feet)	16 x 9 x 8	16 x 9 x 8	16 x 9 x 8	17 x 9 x 8
Improvements Over Previous Model				
Armor	n.a.	n.a.	n.a.	Provisions for bolt-on armor
Other	n.a.	Diesel engine	Enhanced engine cooling Improved suspension	Antispall liner[a] Greater horsepower diesel engine Improved transmission Automotive-type steering and brake controls

Source: Congressional Budget Office based on data from the Department of the Army; Gary W. Cooke, "Gary's Combat Vehicle Reference Guide," available at www.inetres.com/gp/military/cv/index.html; and Christopher Foss, ed., *Jane's Armour and Artillery, 1979-1980* (New York: Wyatt Publishing, 1979).

Note: mpg = miles per gallon; n.a. = not applicable.

a.   The liner protects vehicle occupants from hull fragments.

Table A-4.

Characteristics of Models of the M109 Self-Propelled Howitzer

	Model	
	A2/A3/A4/A5	A6 (Paladin)
Date of Introduction	1962 (Original M109)	1992
Combat Weight (Tons)	28	32
Range (Miles)	217	186
Fuel		
Capacity (Gallons)	135	133
Efficiency (mpg)	1.6	1.4
Size of Cannon (Millimeters)	155	155
Dimensions (Length x width x height, in feet)	30 x 10 x 11	32 x 10 x 11
Improvements Over Previous Model		
Armor	n.a.	Supplemental armor
Other	n.a.	Antispall liner[a] Onboard ballistic computer Improved suspension Enhanced engine cooling Driver's night-vision device

Source: Congressional Budget Office based on data from the Department of the Army and Gary W. Cooke, "Gary's Combat Vehicle Reference Guide," available at www.inetres.com/gp/military/cv/index.html.

Note: mpg = miles per gallon; n.a. = not applicable.

a. The liner protects vehicle occupants from hull fragments.

CBO's Methods for Estimating Airlift Requirements

The Congressional Budget Office (CBO) relied primarily on planning factors developed by the Air Force to estimate the number of airlift sorties needed to deploy Army units overseas.[1] Using the Air Force's planned fleet of 180 C-17s as its basis, CBO estimated how long it would take the Air Force to deliver units' equipment under two conditions—first, to areas where extensive airport facilities would support an unlimited number of daily sorties, and second, to regions of the world where airport facilities were more limited.

Unconstrained Airlift Operations

The delivery of cargo to a theater with extensive airport and aircraft-handling facilities would be limited only by the capacity of the transport fleet to deliver cargo. That is, if the receiving airport was big enough and had enough aircraft-servicing capability to handle hundreds of aircraft at one time, then the amount of cargo that could be delivered in one day would be determined by the number of sorties that an airlift fleet could generate. Under the assumptions of the Air Force's planning factors, the number of sorties that a fleet can generate per day is equal to the number of aircraft in the fleet (#AC) times the number of hours each aircraft will fly, on average, per day (which is referred to as the utilization—UTE—rate), divided by the time needed to fly to and from the destination (round-trip flying time, or RTFT; see Equation 1).[2]

Equation 1:

$$\text{Number of sorties per day} = \frac{(\#AC) \times (\text{UTE rate})}{\text{RTFT}}$$

CBO estimates that the round-trip flying time for deploying units from Savannah, Georgia, to Djibouti in East Africa (the example destination used in the text of this report) is roughly 40 hours.[3] For surge conditions—those that might apply for the first 45 days of a military operation—the Air Force uses a C-17 UTE rate of 14.5 hours per day; for sustained operations, it uses a daily planning value of 12.5 hours.[4] If Djibouti's airfields were sufficiently large, the programmed C-17 fleet—under the assumption of the Air Force's planning values—could deliver 65 sorties per day to Djibouti in surge conditions or 56 sorties per day in a sustained-operations condition, CBO estimates.

Constrained Airlift Operations

In operations that deliver cargo to locations whose airfield facilities are limited, two factors determine the maximum number of daily airlift sorties: the maximum number of aircraft that can be serviced on the ground at one time (MOG) and the amount of time that an aircraft spends on the ground at the destination airport (GT). Based on the relationship used by the Air Force, the number of daily sorties that can be supported by an airfield with limited capacity is equal to the MOG times the number of hours per day that the airfield is in operation

1. Department of the Air Force, Air Mobility Command, *Air Mobility Planning Factors*, Pamphlet 10-1403 (December 18, 2003). That material is also available at www.e-publishing.af.mil/pubfiles/af/10/afpam10-1403/afpam10-1403.pdf.

2. Ibid., p. 4.

3. Although the direct distance is 6,700 nautical miles and the C-17 has an average cruising speed of about 400 knots, such an aircraft cannot fly the entire distance nonstop when carrying a full payload. The time needed to make the full trip includes that of several legs—each of which is less than 4,500 nautical miles—between major Air Force facilities.

4. Department of the Air Force, Air Mobility Command, *Air Mobility Planning Factors*, Table 6.

Table B-1.

CBO's Estimates of Maximum Airfield Capacity

Maximum Number of Aircraft on Ground	Number of C-17 Sorties	
	24-Hour Operations	Daylight Operations[a]
1	6	4
2	13	8
3	19	13
4	25	17

Source: Congressional Budget Office based on Department of the Air Force, *Air Mobility Planning Factors,* Pamphlet 10-1403 (December 18, 2003), Table 8.

Note: The numbers incorporate the Air Force's planning factors: ground time equals 3.25 hours, and efficiency equals 85 percent.

c. Sixteen hours per day.

(OH) times the queuing efficiency at the airfield (Eff) divided by the average time spent on the ground (GT; see Equation 2).

Equation 2:
Number of sorties per day = $\dfrac{(MOG) \times (OH) \times (Eff)}{(GT)}$

For airlift operations into Djibouti, CBO made several assumptions that are consistent with the Air Force's planning factors:[5]

■ The airfield would operate (=OH) 24 hours a day during the first 45 days of an operation and only during daylight hours—assumed to be 16 hours per day—after the first 45 days;

■ Queuing efficiency (Eff) would equal 85 percent; and

■ Ground time (GT) would equal 3.25 hours for C-17 deliveries.

CBO also assumed that the Djibouti airfield would have a MOG value of three, which would be fairly typical for a country with such a poorly developed infrastructure.[6] Using those values, CBO estimated that the Air Force would be able to process 19 C-17 sorties per day through the Djibouti airport by operating 24 hours a day in surge conditions but in sustained operations would be able to handle only 13 sorties per day (see Table B-1).

5. Ibid., Tables 5 and 8.

6. See the entry on Djibouti in the Central Intelligence Agency's *The World Factbook*, available at www.cia.gov/cia/publications/factbook/index.html; and Congressional Budget Office, *Options for Restructuring the Army* (May 2005), Appendix C.

Definitions of Technology Readiness Levels and Assessments of Critical Technologies for the Army's Future Combat Systems Program

The National Aeronautics and Space Administration has developed a scheme of technology readiness levels (TRLs) that measures the progress of development in space programs. Using a scale of 1 to 9, the levels refer to technologies that range from those existing only on paper to those that have been demonstrated in operational tests in typical mission conditions (see Table C-1). The Department of Defense has adopted those measures to assess the technological readiness of defense programs, and the Army has used them to evaluate a number of technologies (ranging from 31 to 54, depending on when they were measured) that it considers critical to developing its Future Combat Systems (FCS).

The Army has conducted several assessments of the readiness of the technologies that it considers critical to FCS development since the beginning of 2003 (see Table C-2 on page 77 and Table C-3 on page 78). The first one, which identified 31 critical technologies, was conducted at about the time that the FCS program entered the system development and demonstration phase in the spring of 2003. Subsequent assessments were made in the fall of 2004 by the FCS program manager's office and by an independent team assembled by the Deputy Assistant Secretary of the Army for Research and Technology.[1] By that time, the 31 critical technology areas had been expanded into 54 more specific critical technologies. In April 2005 an assessment update was conducted by Deputy Assistant Secretary of the Army for Research and Technology.[2] Between the October 2004 and the April 2005 assessment updates, the number of critical technologies had been reduced to 49, the Army having concluded that five of the previously identified 54 critical technologies were no longer needed to develop the FCS components prior to initial fielding.

---

1. Office of the Deputy Assistant Secretary of the Army for Research and Technology, *Future Combat Systems (FCS) Increment 1 Technology Readiness Assessment (TRA) Update* (October 2004).

2. Office of the Deputy Assistant Secretary of the Army for Research and Technology, *Technology Readiness Assessment Update* (April 2005).

Table C-1.

Definitions and Descriptions of Technology Readiness Levels

Technology Readiness Level	Description	Hardware and Software	Demonstration Environment
1. Basic Principles Observed and Reported	At lowest level of technology readiness, scientific research begins to be translated into applied research and development Examples might include paper studies of a technology's basic properties	None (Paper studies and analysis)	None
2. Technology Concept or Application Formulated	Invention begins—once basic principles are observed, practical applications can be invented The application is speculative, and there is no proof or detailed analysis to support the assumption Examples are still limited to paper studies	None (Paper studies and analysis)	None
3. Analytical and Experimental Critical Function or Characteristic Proof of Concept	Active research and development is initiated, including analytical and laboratory studies to physically validate analytical predictions of separate elements of the technology Examples include components that are not yet integrated or representative	Analytical studies and demonstration of nonscale individual components (Portions of subsystems)	Laboratory
4. Component or "Breadboard" Validation in a Laboratory Environment	Basic technological components are integrated to establish that the pieces will work together (relatively "low fidelity" compared with the eventual system) Examples include integration of "ad hoc" hardware in a laboratory	Low-fidelity breadboard Integration of nonscale components to show that pieces will work together Pieces are not fully functional in form or fit but representative of technically feasible approach suitable for fielded systems	Laboratory

Continued

Table C-1.

Continued

- -

Technology Readiness Level	Description	Hardware and Software	Demonstration Environment
5. Component or Breadboard Validation in a Relevant Environment	Fidelity of breadboard technology increases significantly The basic technological components are integrated with reasonably realistic supporting elements so that the technology can be tested in a simulated environment Examples include "high-fidelity" laboratory integration of components	"High-fidelity" breadboard The technology is functionally equivalent but not necessarily final in form or fit (size, weight, materials, and so forth) Components should be approaching appropriate scale The level may include integration of several components with reasonably realistic supporting elements or subsystems to demonstrate functionality	Laboratory for demonstrating functionality but not form and fit May include demonstrating breadboard in surrogate vehicle The technology is ready for detailed design studies
6. System/Subsystem Model or Prototype Demonstration in a Relevant Environment	A representative model or prototype system, which is well beyond the breadboard tested for TRL 5, is tested in a relevant environment representing a major step up in a technology's demonstrated readiness Examples include testing a prototype in a "high-fidelity" laboratory environment or simulated operational environment	The prototype should be very close to final in form, fit, and function and should probably integrate many new components and realistic supporting elements or subsystems if needed to demonstrate full functionality of the elements or subsystem	"High-fidelity" laboratory demonstration or limited/restricted flight or road demonstration in a relevant environment Integration of the technology is well defined
7. System Prototype Demonstration in an Operational Environment	The prototype is near or at the level of the planned operational system This level represents a major step up from TRL 6, requiring the demonstration of an actual system prototype in an operational environment, such as in an aircraft or vehicle or in space Examples include testing the prototype in a test-bed vehicle	The prototype should be integrated with other key supporting elements or subsystems to demonstrate the full functionality of the element or subsystem	Demonstration in a representative operational environment, such as a test-bed or demonstrator vehicle Technology is well substantiated with test data

- -

Continued

Table C-1.

Continued

Technology Readiness Level	Description	Hardware and Software	Demonstration Environment
8. Actual System Completed and "Flight or Field Qualified" Through Test and Demonstration	The technology has been proven to work in its final form and under expected conditions In almost all cases, this TRL represents the end of true system development Examples include developmental test and evaluation of the system in its intended weapon structure to determine if it meets design specifications	Field-qualified hardware	Developmental test and evaluation in the actual system application
9. Actual System "Flight or Field Proven" Through Successful Mission Operations	The technology is applied in its final form and under mission conditions, such as those encountered in operational test and evaluation In almost all cases, this is the end of the last "bug fixing" aspects of true system development Examples include operating the system under mission conditions	Actual system in final form	Operational test and evaluation in mission conditions

Source: Government Accountability Office, *Defense Acquisitions: Improved Business Case Is Needed for Future Combat System's Successful Outcome,* GAO-06-367 (March 2006), p. 49.

Table C-2.

Technology Readiness Levels of Critical Technologies for the FCS Program in May 2003

	Technology Readiness Level in May 2003[a]	Component for Which Technology Is Needed
Software Programmable Radio	6	Network
Interface and Information Exchange	4.5	Network
Security Systems and Algorithms	5.5	Network
Mobile Ad Hoc Networking Protocols	6	Network
Quality of Service Algorithms	5	Network
Unmanned Systems Relay	6	UAVs
Wideband Waveforms	5	Network
Advanced Man-Machine Interfaces	6	Network
Multispectral Sensors and Seekers	5.5	Network
Decision Aids and Intelligent Agents	6	Network
Combat Identification	5.5	Network
Rapid Battlespace Deconfliction	6	Network
Sensor/Data Fusion and Data Compression Algorithms	4.5	Network
Dynamic Sensor-Shooter Pairing Algorithms and Fire Control	5	Network
Line-of-Sight/Beyond-Line-of-Sight/Non-Line-of-Sight (Terminal guidance)	5	MGVs, NLOS-LS
Aided and Automatic Target Recognition	5.5	UGVs, Network, NLOS-LS
Recoil Management and Lightweight Components	4	MGVs
Distributive Collaboration of Manned/Unmanned Platforms	5	UGVs
Rapid Battle Damage Assessment	4	No longer required[b]
High-Power Density/Fuel-Efficient Propulsion	5	MGVs
Embedded Predictive Logistics Sensors and Algorithms	5.5	MGVs, UGVs, UAVs
Water Generation and Purification	5.5	No longer required[b]
Computer-Generated Forces	6	Network, MGVs
Tactical Engagement Simulation	5	Network, MGVs
Active Protection System	5	MGVs
Signature Management	5	MGVs
Lightweight Hull and Vehicle Armor	5.5	UGVs, MGVs
Health Monitoring and Casualty Care Interventions	8	Network, MGVs
Power Distribution and Control	5	UGVs, MGVs
Advanced Countermine Technology	4.5	Network, MGVs, UGVs
High-Density Packaged Power	5.5	UGVs, MGVs

Source: Congressional Budget Office based on data from the Department of the Army.

Notes: FCS = Future Combat Systems; UAV = unmanned aerial vehicle; NLOS-LS = non-line-of-sight launch system; UGV = unmanned ground vehicle; MGV = manned ground vehicle.

a.   Assessment by the Deputy Assistant Secretary of the Army for Research and Technology.

b.   No longer required for initial fielding of FCS components.

Table C-3.

Status of Critical Technologies for the FCS Program As Assessed After May 2003

	Technology Readiness Assessments (TRL)				Projected Attainment of TRL 6				Component for Which Technology Is Needed
	Oct. 2004 Program Manager	IRT	DAS (R&T) April 2005	Program Manager May 2006	Oct. 2004 Program Manager	IRT	DAS (R&T) April 2005	Program Manager May 2006	
Software Programmable Radio									
JTRS Cluster 1	5	5	5	6	2006	2006	2007	2006	Network
JTRS Cluster 5	5	5	5	6	2006	2006	2007	2006	Network
WIN-T	5	5	5	6	2006	2006	2007	2006	Network
Interface and Information Exchange									
Army, joint, multinational interface	4	4	4	6	2006	2007+	2008	2006	Network
WIN-T strategic communication	4	4	4	6	2006	2007+	2008	2006	Network
Security Systems and Algorithms									
Cross-domain guarding solution	3	3	4	6	2006	2007+	2008	2006	Network
Intrusion detection—Internet protocol	5	5	4	4	2006	2007+	2008	2008	Network
Intrusion detection—network waveform	3	3	4	4	2006	2007+	2007	2007	Network
Mobile Ad Hoc Networking Protocols	5	5	5	5	2006	2007+	2007	2007	Network
Quality of Service Algorithms	5	5	5	5	2006	2007+	2007	2008	Network
Unmanned Systems Relay	5	5	5	n.r.	2006	2006	2006	n.r.	UAVs
Wideband Waveforms									
JTRS	5	5	5	6	2006	2007+	2007	2006	Network
Soldier radio waveform	4	4	4	6	2006	2007+	2007	2006	Network
Advanced Man-Machine Interfaces	6	5	6	6	2006	2006	2005	2005	Network
Multispectral Sensors and Seekers	6	6	6	6	2006	2006	2005	2005	Network
Decision Aids and Intelligent Agents	6	6	6	6	2006	2006	2005	2005	Network
Combat Identification									
Air (rotary wing/UAV)-to-ground	6	6	6	6	2006	2006	2005	2005	Network
Air (fixed wing)-to-ground	4	4	NLR	NLR	2007+	2006	NLR	NLR	n.a.
Ground-to-air	3	3	NLR	NLR	2007+	2006	NLR	NLR	n.a.
Ground-to-ground (Mounted)	6	6	6	6	2006	2006	2005	2005	Network
Ground-to-soldier	4	4	NLR	NLR	2007+	2006	NLR	NLR	n.a.
Rapid Battlespace Deconfliction	5	5	5	5	2006	2007+	2008	2009	Network
Sensor/Data Fusion and Data Compression Algorithms									
Distributed fusion management	4	4	4	4	2006	2007+	2007	2007	Network
Level 1 fusion engine	6	6	6	6	2006	2007+	2005	2005	Network
Data-compression algorithms	6	6	6	6	2006	2007+	2005	2005	Network
Dynamic Sensor-Shooter Pairing Algorithms and Fire Control	6	5.5	5	6	2006	2006	2006	2006	Network
Line-of-Sight/Beyond-Line-of-Sight/Non-Line-of-Sight (Terminal guidance)									
Precision-guided mortar munitions	5	5	5	6	2006	n.r.	2007	2006	MGVs
Multirole precision munitions	6	4.5	5	6	2006	n.r.	2007	2006	MGVs
Excalibur precision munitions	5	5.5	6	6	2006	n.r.	2005	2005	MGVs
Non-line-of-sight launch system	6	5	6	6	2006	n.r.	2005	2005	NLOS-LS
Aided and Automatic Target Recognition									
Aided target recognition for reconnaissance, surveillance, and target acquisition	5	5	5	5	2006	2006	2007	2008	UGVs
Non-line-of-sight launch system aided target recognition for seekers	6	5	6	6	2006	2006	2005	2005	Network, NLOS-LS

Continued

Table C-3.

Continued

	Technology Readiness Assessments (TRL)				Projected Attainment of TRL 6				Component for Which Technology Is Needed
	Oct. 2004		DAS (R&T) April 2005	Program Manager May 2006	Oct. 2004		DAS (R&T) April 2005	Program Manager May 2006	
	Program Manager	IRT			Program Manager	IRT			
Recoil Management and Lightweight Components	5	5	6	6	2006	2007+	2005	2005	MGVs
Distributive Collaboration of Manned/Unmanned Platforms	5	5	5	5	2006	2006	2006	2006	UGVs
Rapid Battle Damage Assessment	3	4	NLR	NLR	2007+	2007+	NLR	NLR	n.a.
High-Power Density/Fuel-Efficient Propulsion									
High-power density engine	5	5	5	6	2006	2006	2007	2006	MGVs
Fuel-efficient hybrid-electric engine	6	6	6	6	2006	2006	2005	2005	MGVS
Embedded Predictive Logistics Sensors and Algorithms	2	4.5	5	n.r.	2007+	2007+	2008	n.r.	MGVs, UGVs, UAVs
Water Generation and Purification	5	5	NLR	NLR	2007+	2007+	NLR	NLR	n.a.
Computer Generated Forces	6	6	6	6	2006	2006	2005	2005	Network, MGVs
Tactical Engagement Simulation	4	4	4[a]	5	2006	2007+	2008	2008	Network, MGVs
Active Protection System									
Active protection system	6	6	5	6	2006	2006	2008	2006	MGVs
Threat warning system	4	4.5	4	4.5	2007+	2007+	2009	2009	MGVs
Signature Management	5	5.5	5	6	2006	2006	2006	2006	MGVs
Lightweight Hull and Vehicle Armor	5	5	5	5	2006	2007+	2008	2008	UGVs, MGVs
Health Monitoring and Casualty Care Interventions	8	6	6	6	2005	2006	2005	2005	Network, MGVs
Power Distribution and Control	5	5	5	6	2006	2006	2006	2006	UGVs, MGVs
Advanced Countermine Technology									
Mine detection	6	6	6	6	2006	n.r.	2005	2005	Network, UGVs
Mine neutralization	6	6	6	6	2006	n.r.	2005	2005	UGVs
Efficient resource allocation	6	6	6	n.r.	2006	n.r.	2005	n.a.	Network, UGVs
Protection	4	4	4	4	2007+	n.r.	2008	2008	MGVs
High-Density Packaged Power	5	5	5	6	2006	2006	2008	2006	UGVs, MGVs
Class 1 UAV Propulsion Technology									
Ducted fan	4	4	4[b]	6	2006	2006	2005	2005	UAVs
Lightweight heavy-fuel engine	3	3	4	5	2006	2006	2007	2006	UAVs

Source: Congressional Budget Office based on data from the Department of the Army; Deputy Assistant Secretary of the Army for Research and Technology, *Future Combat Systems (FCS) Increment 1 Technology Readiness Assessment (TRA) Update* (October 2004); and Deputy Assistant Secretary of the Army for Research and Technology, *Technology Readiness Update Assessment* (April 2005).

Notes: FCS = Future Combat Systems; DAS (R&T) = Deputy Assistant Secretary of the Army for Research and Technology; IRT = Independent Review Team; JTRS = Joint Tactical Radio System; WIN-T = Warfighting Information Network-Tactical; n.r. = not reported; n.a. = not applicable; UAV = unmanned aerial vehicle; NLR = no longer required for initial fielding of FCS components; MGV = manned ground vehicle; NLOS-LS = non-line-of-sight launch system; UGV = unmanned ground vehicle.

a. Upgraded to TRL 5 by the Army in January 2006 on the basis of tests conducted in the fall of 2005.

b. Upgraded to TRL 6 by the Army in January 2006 on the basis of tests conducted in August 2005.

Methods Used to Estimate Costs

To estimate the costs of the alternatives considered in this analysis, the Congressional Budget Office (CBO) had to establish the costs of individual components of the Future Combat Systems (FCS) program and the associated network as well as the costs of upgrades to existing weapon systems. This appendix describes the methods that CBO used to assess the research and development (R&D) and procurement costs of the FCS components and network and the costs of upgrades. It also briefly discusses the risk that costs may grow beyond their original estimates over the life of the program.

Estimating Costs of FCS Components

The Department of Defense (DoD) submits annual Selected Acquisition Reports (SARs) to the Congress that provide estimates of costs for major weapons programs. The SARs for the FCS program provide separate estimates of the total R&D and total procurement costs for the program's first increment (that is, the first 15 brigades' worth of equipment). On the basis of those reports, CBO developed independent estimates of the costs of individual FCS components, separating those expenditures into R&D and procurement costs.

Research and Development Costs

Total R&D costs for the FCS program, according to the Army's latest estimates, are projected to be $29 billion (in 2006 dollars).[1] CBO apportioned those costs to the various types of systems—such as manned ground vehicles or unmanned aerial vehicles (UAVs)—on the basis of spending planned by the Army for 2005 through 2011. Under those plans, manned vehicles would account for about 20 percent of total R&D costs; UAVs would account for 2 percent; unmanned ground vehicles, for 3 percent; the non-line-of-sight launch system (NLOS-LS), for 5 per-

cent; and unmanned ground sensors and the intelligent munitions system together, for 1 percent. CBO assumed that 20 percent of R&D costs would be spent on program management and that the remainder, about 50 percent, would go toward software and network development and systems integration. In developing the costs of the various alternatives it considered, CBO attributed portions of those management, development, and integration costs to individual systems on the basis of a system's share of total R&D costs.

Procurement Costs

CBO estimated the portion of the procurement costs for each brigade's worth of FCS equipment that could be assigned to individual systems or groups of systems. According to recent FCS SARs, the total cost of procuring 15 brigades' worth of FCS components would be about $100 billion, or an average unit cost of $6.7 billion. The average unit cost covers more than 800 individual systems—including manned vehicles, UAVs, and unmanned ground vehicles—and the network. CBO used several different methods to estimate the costs for procuring the various components of the FCS-equipped brigades.

Manned Vehicles. The costs of manned vehicles make up the bulk of the costs associated with an FCS-equipped brigade. All told, 322 manned vehicles would be needed to equip an FCS brigade; an additional 11 vehicles would be required as spares (known as "operational float").[2] In assessing the costs of the eight different manned FCS vehicles, CBO combined a cost-estimating relationship (CER) developed by Technomics and the Army's Cost and Economic Analysis Center with the previously esti-

---

1. These costs include the total estimated R&D costs for the FCS program for the years from 2003 through 2016.

2. Quantities are based on those in Logistics Requirements and Readiness IPT, Materiel Fielding Sub-IPT, of the Boeing/SAIC Lead Systems Integrator, *Future Combat Systems (FCS): Equipped Unit of Action (UA) Materiel Fielding Plan (MFP) to the UA Supportability Strategy* (April 2005), pp. 27 and 57.

mated costs of the Crusader artillery system.[3] (The CER relates the cost of manned armored vehicles to their characteristics—such as speed, armament, and passenger capacity—as well as to the year in which the vehicle is first produced.)[4] CBO also used the estimated costs of the Crusader to determine a unit cost for the proposed non-line-of-sight cannon and to calibrate the estimates derived from the CER.[5] Using those methods, CBO estimated that the manned vehicles would account for $4.2 billion (63 percent) of the total cost of a brigade's worth of FCS equipment.

Unmanned Ground and Aerial Vehicles. CBO relied primarily on the Army's estimates of the unit costs of unmanned ground vehicles, which ranged from $1 million to $5 million.[6] On the basis of those costs, CBO estimated that the total cost of unmanned FCS ground vehicles for a brigade would account for roughly $700 million (10 percent) of the total cost of a brigade's worth of equipment.

For the most part, CBO estimated the costs of UAVs by using CERs developed by Technomics for the Deputy Assistant Secretary of the Army for Cost and Economics.[7] Separate CERs were used to determine the cost of the aerial vehicle and the ground station associated with each class of UAVs. Again, estimates obtained using the CERs were compared with estimates of existing systems and adjusted as necessary. The resultant total cost of the UAVs (which would number more than 200 in each brigade under the Administration's plan) and accompanying launch

units, according to CBO's estimates, would account for $350 million (5 percent) of the total costs of FCS equipment for one brigade.

Remaining Unattended Systems. Cost estimates that CBO developed for the three remaining weapon systems—unattended ground sensors, the NLOS-LS, and the improved munitions system—were all based on the costs of existing systems or systems in development:

■ Unit costs for the ground sensors were based loosely on those for REMBASS II—the Army's remotely monitored battlefield sensor system;

■ Costs for the NLOS-LS were based on those for the high-mobility advanced rocket system (HIMARS) launcher; costs for the NLOS-LS munitions, on those for the guided rockets for the multiple launch rocket system (GMLRS); and

■ Costs for the improved munitions system were based on those of the Spider smart-mine system.

Total costs for equipping a brigade with those systems would be roughly $300 million, or 5 percent of the costs for equipping it with all FCS components.

The Network. The remainder of the costs to procure a brigade's worth of FCS components would be approximately $1.1 billion, in CBO's estimation, or 17 percent of the total. CBO assumed that those costs could be attributed to the network.

Basis for Estimates of Cost Growth
CBO based its estimates of the potential for growth in the costs of FCS components largely on research conducted by the RAND Corporation. RAND has compiled a database covering cost growth from 1969 to 1999 for all major programs for which DoD submitted annual SARs to the Congress during that period.[8] (The database includes 3,047 SARs for 274 programs.) Analysts compared

---

3. The Crusader program was canceled in 2002.

4. Steve Pawlow, Army Cost and Economic Analysis Center, and Jeff Cherwonik and Paul Hardin, Technomics, "Ground Vehicle Procurement Cost Estimating Methodology," presented at the 35th DoD Cost Analysis Symposium, Williamsburg, Va., January 2002.

5. Estimates of costs for the Crusader system were based on Government Accountability Office, *Army Armored Systems: Meeting Crusader Requirements Will Be a Technical Challenge,* GAO/NSIAD-97-121 (June 1997); and Office of the Undersecretary of Defense for Acquisition and Technology, Selected Acquisition Report Summary Tables, December 31, 1997.

6. Private correspondence provided by the Army to the Congressional Budget Office.

7. Technomics and the Office of the Deputy Assistant Secretary of the Army for Cost and Economics, "Unmanned Aerial Vehicle System Acquisition Cost Estimating Methodology," presented at the 37th DoD Cost Analysis Symposium, Williamsburg, Va., February 2004.

---

8. At the time this analysis was prepared, the most recent RAND publication based on its SAR database was Jeanne M. Jarvaise, Jeffrey A. Drezner, and D. Norton, *The Defense System Cost Performance Database: Cost Growth Analysis Using Selected Acquisition Reports,* MR-625-OSD (Santa Monica, Calif.: RAND, 1996). The estimates of cost growth that CBO used for its analysis are based on unpublished updates of that report prepared in 1999 through 2002 by Robert S. Leonard, Fred Timson, and John C. Graser.

Table D-1.

Rates of Historical Cost Growth for Military Systems

(Percent)

Type of System	Research, Development, Testing, and Evaluation	Procurement
Command, Control, Communications, and Intelligence	69	19
Ground Combat Vehicles	71	74
Missiles and Munitions	45	35
Unmanned Aerial Vehicles	42	23

Source: Congressional Budget Office based on analysis by RAND.

Note: The growth of total development or procurement costs is measured from the estimates made of such costs when the system enters the system development and demonstration phase.

DoD's estimates of costs for those programs at Milestone B (entry into the system development and demonstration phase)—when extensive development activity begins—with DoD's estimates for the systems' costs once they had gone into production and become operational.[9] RAND developed estimates of increases or decreases in development and procurement costs for eight categories of systems, including ships, ground combat vehicles, and aircraft, breaking down the data by service and type of weapon.[10]

RAND's analysis suggests that most DoD weapons programs increase in cost.[11] However, R&D and procurement costs for Army ground combat vehicles have experi-

enced some of the highest growth rates—both types of costs have risen by more than 70 percent relative to early estimates. Other systems being developed in the FCS program have experienced cost growth at lower rates, according to RAND (see Table D-1).

To determine an overall potential for cost growth for the Administration's FCS program and for the alternatives presented in this study, CBO applied the rate relevant for each kind of system to the R&D and procurement costs allotted to the various portions of the FCS program. CBO estimates the potential for cost growth in the planned FCS program to be 67 percent for the R&D portion and roughly 60 percent for the cost to procure 15 brigades' worth of FCS components.

Estimates of Costs to Upgrade Current Systems

The modernization of current systems that CBO considered in its analysis was basically of two types: upgrades of systems to a more recent model or the incorporation of FCS technology into an existing system. In general, CBO relied on the Army's estimates of the costs for such modernization. Some of the Army's estimates are based on upgrades that have been made to existing systems for several years. (For example, the Army has been upgrading older models of its M1 Abrams tanks to the M1A2 model for more than 10 years.) The Army has also assessed the costs for upgrading current systems with FCS technologies;

---

9. Major DoD programs go through a series of stages that are outlined in DoD's acquisition regulations. Milestone B (formerly Milestone II) represents a program's entrance into the system development and demonstration stage. A discussion of those milestones and stages is included in DoD Instruction 5000.2, dated May 12, 2003, available at www.dtic.mil/whs/directives/corres/pdf2/i50002p.pdf.

10. The Institute for Defense Analyses (IDA) has also analyzed trends in weapons costs using a database constructed from DoD's Selected Acquisition Reports. Like RAND, IDA produced separate estimates for the different military services and for various types of systems, but it used slightly different methods in estimating cost growth—adjusting for model changes as well as for changes in total quantity—and its estimates covered a somewhat different group of systems. Nonetheless, its estimates of past cost growth mostly equal or exceed those reported by RAND. See Karen W. Tyson and others, *The Effects of Management Initiatives on the Costs and Schedules of Defense Acquisition Programs* (Alexandria, Va.: Institute for Defense Analyses, 1992); and Karen W. Tyson, Bruce R. Harmon, and Daniel M. Utech, *Understanding Cost and Schedule Growth in Acquisition Programs* (Alexandria, Va.: Institute for Defense Analyses, 1994).

11. For additional discussion of cost growth in DoD programs, see Congressional Budget Office, *The Long-Term Implications of Current Defense Plans* (January 2003), pp. 44-46.

such costs ranged from $700,000 per upgraded M113 to $8 million per upgraded Abrams tank.

Like the costs for other aspects of the FCS program, those for inserting FCS technology into existing systems could experience growth by the time the upgrades are actually carried out. Therefore, CBO applied likely rates of growth to those portions of the upgrade costs that would apply to FCS components. The rates were based on those experienced in programs to upgrade the Abrams tank and Bradley fighting vehicle from 1994 to 2003 and averaged 50 percent.[12]

---

12. See Office of the Principal Deputy Undersecretary of Defense for Acquisition Technology and Logistics, "Remanufacture of Defense Systems: Case Studies of Cost Experiences and Lessons for Future Programs" (November 2001), presented at the 35th DoD Cost Analysis Symposium, Williamsburg, Va., January 2002.